U-BOATS

off the

OUTER BANKS

Shadows in the Moonlight

JIM BUNCH

THE
History
PRESS

Published by The History Press
Charleston, SC
www.historypress.net

Copyright © 2017 by Jim Bunch
All rights reserved

Front cover, bottom: *U-85* is sunk by the *Roper*. *Glen Eure painting.*

First published 2017

Manufactured in the United States

ISBN 9781467137676

Library of Congress Control Number: 2017934929

For my partner in life, Beverlee Lynn Kearns, and my son, Mike Bunch

CONTENTS

FOREWORD

J im W. Bunch's book holds a particular and personal fascination for me. Born on the island of Oahu in the then Territory of Hawaii, I witnessed the Japanese attack on Pearl Harbor. With the possibility of invasion looming, my mother, sister and I were among civilians evacuated on an ocean liner with destroyer escort in early 1942. We settled at the Eure family home in Swansboro, North Carolina, and I can remember, as a lad there, seeing ships burning on the horizon.

North Carolina was definitely experiencing the reverberation of Pearl Harbor across the Pacific to the Atlantic coastline of the United States. With Germany's declaration of war in support of its allies and the resulting lifting of restrictions on attacking American vessels, it began implementation of its long-planned and devastating coastal U-boat war.

The author's concentration on the seven months of U-boat activity along the Outer Banks of North Carolina includes a visualization of coastal communities as they existed during the first half of 1942. It is both fascinating and illuminating in showing the proximity of places like Kitty Hawk, Nags Had, Oregon Inlet and Hatteras to ships sunk off their shores.

Bunch is a celebrated oceanographer, historian and diver who has done extensive exploration of *U-85* off Oregon Inlet and guided many to this historic wreck. His dives on the *U-85*, *U-352* and *U-701* total close to one thousand over the past forty years. In this new book, he combines his skills and research to take the readers on a different journey—this one a studied and detailed account of all coastal North Carolina U-boat activity during the period, the boats and individuals involved and the ultimate impact.

U-Boats off the Outer Banks: Shadows in the Moonlight puts the *U-85* experience in a historical perspective and is a natural development of his earlier volumes of *Diving the U-85* and *Germany's U-85: A Shadow in the Sea*. I am pleased to add this book to my Bunch collection, which enables me in my ninth decade to still travel under water as well as back in time.

—Glen Eure, Major, U.S. Army (retired)

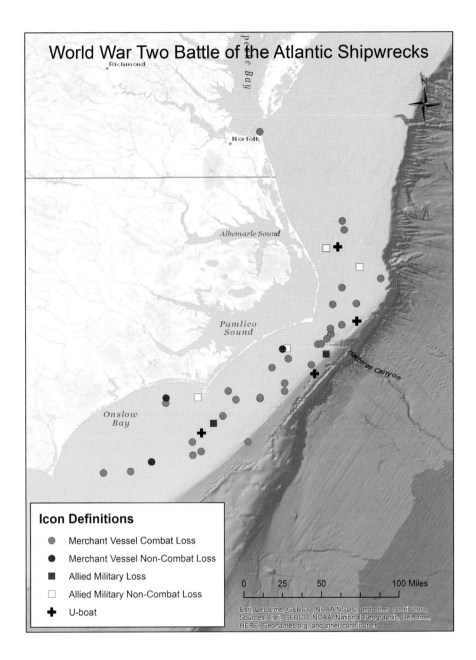

Map of the Battle of the Atlantic off the North Carolina coast. *Courtesy of NOAA.*

PREFACE

During the first seven months of 1942, people living along the beaches of coastal North Carolina were closer to World War II than most of our overseas forces. Even today, it's still a surprise to many visitors how close the U-boats were and the terrible amount of death and destruction they brought to both men and ships. That's mainly why I wrote this book: to let folks know and hopefully not forget just what went on along the North Carolina coast during the first seven months of 1942.

Over the last fifty years, I have visited many of these shipwrecks personally as a scuba diver, over forty of them in all. Logging somewhere around six thousand dives out there, I felt somehow a part of all the death and destruction that went on. Each shipwreck was different and had its own story to tell. Most were the victims of U-boats, and four of these silent hunters that became the hunted occupy their place on the sandy bottom too. They're all still out there, the hunters and hunted alike, but they're rusting away and will soon be only memories like so many of the divers and captains I went to sea with are already.

Now for some deserved thanks. Working with the images found in this book was quite a job, and the help given me by Keith and Barbara Newsome, Mary Ellen Riddle, Ed Caram, Wolfgang Klue, Bill Palmer, Joe Hoyt, the History Center in Manteo, John Finelli and Gary Gentile is greatly appreciated.

On a personal note, the inspiration given me by my son, Mike Bunch, and partner in life for over thirty years, Beverly Kearns, made it possible for me to complete this book. Their memory will always be a part of it.

INTRODUCTION

On January 18, 1942, about sixty miles off the coast of Cape Hatteras, the Standard Oil Company's tanker *Allen Jackson* moved northward through a calm sea. The 4,038-ton ship was loaded with 72,870 barrels of crude oil bound for New York. It was about one thirty in the morning, and most of the thirty-five-man crew, including the captain, were asleep in their bunks. They were not alone.

Several miles to the northeast of the approaching tanker and waiting on the surface was Fregattenakapitan Richard Zapp and his *U-66*. He would not need to wait very long. With all lights blazing and not tacking, the *Allen Jackson* was doomed.

Two torpedoes hit the *Jackson*, and the burning oil lit up the night sky as if daylight had suddenly dawned. The ship broke in two and soon went down. Twenty-two of the thirty-five men on board would not see the light of day. The war at sea had begun off the North Carolina coast.

Over the next seven months, no fewer than seventy-five ships would sink to the bottom in North Carolina's Graveyard of the Atlantic. World War II would go on for almost three more years, but the battle off the North Carolina coast against the U-boats virtually ended in mid-July 1942. This is the story of what went on during these first seven months of that war on and off the coast of North Carolina.

CHAPTER 1

THE GERMAN PLAN

Operation Drumbeat

Germany had been at war with Great Britain for two long years. At Admiral Karl Donitz's headquarters, which at that time was located on an estuary near the U-boat pens at Lorient, a man sat at his desk and was formulating a plan that would change the course of the war. Donitz was the chief of U-boat operations, and his best planner was Victor Oehrn. It was a cold and windy day, but this didn't deter Oehrn from his work. He had planned the October 1939 attack on Scapa Flow that was carried out by Gunther Prien and his *U-47*. This operation was the best-known U-boat action of the war and resulted in the sinking of the British battleship *Royal Oak*. Over 1,200 sailors died when the ship went down. Prien became a national hero and was personally decorated by Hitler. Oehrn received no recognition for the plan, which was ingenious. Donitz took all the credit.

Now it was the fall of 1941 and Oehrn was at it again, this time studying a map of the East Coast of the United States. He knew that this long and mostly unprotected coast was traveled by a large numbers of ships that sailed alone, heading for the convoy lanes of the North Atlantic. If these ships, especially the tankers, could be sunk by his U-boats before reaching the protection of the convoy escorts, it would greatly increase Germany's goal of starving Great Britain of oil.

Oehrn also noticed on these maps that there was one place that stood out as a focus for any coming attack. It was a place where the depth of the ocean quickly dropped off to more than six hundred feet and was far from any known defensive bases. He also knew that the northward-moving Gulf

Admiral Karl Donitz, commander of the German U-boat force, meets a U-boat returning from a war cruise. *Bundesarchiv, Koblenz.*

Stream would cause shipping moving south around the point that reached far out into the ocean there to hug the coast. This place was Cape Hatteras, North Carolina.

Oehrn would be transferred in November 1941 to a new job in Rome, but his planning for the upcoming offensive along the East Coast of the United States would pay handsomely for Karl Donitz and Germany.

In July 1941, German U-boats were still busy attacking British shipping along the North Atlantic convoy routes. Even then, five months before Pearl Harbor, the German naval staff knew that America was determined to do all that was possible to help England win the war. The staff had also concluded, "Thus in effect the United States has become Great Britain's ally without declaring war, and in consequence the odds in the Atlantic have become weighted against us."

Since the spring of 1941, the tempo of American aid had continually increased, and U.S. naval and air forces had extended their activity across the Atlantic. Several U-boats had already been attacked. U-boat command also knew that U.S. warships were helping to escort British Atlantic convoys. This continued to greatly handicap the U-boat campaign. Attacks on darkened escort vessels were still forbidden by Hitler, and the U.S. merchant and naval ships were still immune from attack. Utterly frustrated, the German naval staff even submitted a proposal in September 1941 that action should

Victor Oehrn (*left*). *Bundesarchiv, Koblenz.*

be taken against American vessels carrying supplies to Britain, but it was rejected by Hitler on political grounds.

As more time went by, it became evident that the United States intended to gain as much time as it could before entering a war with Germany. A large part of the American population was still not in favor of another war. U.S. president Franklin Roosevelt realized that international developments pointed to a possible war on two fronts—the Atlantic and Pacific—and that his existing armed forces were inadequate to win such a conflict. As late as September 1941, Roosevelt was still unwilling to start an open battle with Germany. Even a number of incidents in the Atlantic had failed to move the Washington government from its politics.

On September 4, 1941, *U-652* was operating near Iceland. The boat was followed by an American destroyer that dropped three depth charges in an attempt to sink the submarine. *U-652* fired two torpedoes in a defensive act, which the destroyer succeeded in evading. The destroyer was the USS *Greer*.

On September 11, Roosevelt told the American people in a nationwide broadcast that the U-boat had attacked the *Greer* without any provocation and that this was an act of piracy. This proved to be untrue but still didn't convince Hitler to change his policy of nonaggression with respect to America. President Roosevelt made his policy clear in this broadcast:

> There has now come a time when you and I must see the cold, inexorable necessity of saying to these inhuman, unrestrained seekers of world conquest and permanent world domination by the sword: "You seek to throw our children and our children's children into your form of terrorism and slavery. You have now attacked our own safety. You shall go no further."…
>
> When you see a rattlesnake poised to strike, you do not wait until he has struck before you crush him….
>
> In the waters which we deem necessary for our defense, American naval vessels and American planes will no longer wait until Axis submarines lurking under the water, or Axis raiders on the surface of the sea, strike their deadly blow—first.

During the month of October, the reality of a coming war with Germany loomed even closer. U.S. merchant ships were armed, and a German U-boat sank the American destroyer *Reuben James* on October 31 while the *James* was escorting a British convoy. The captain of the *U-552* that sank the destroyer was Erich Topp. It was his contention that it was nighttime and he could not identify the *James* as American. Topp would soon be sinking ships off the North Carolina coast. No formal action was taken by the United States, but since September 4 and the *Greer* incident, the United States was already in a de facto war with Germany.

Soon after this incident, a study by the German naval staff on the prosecution of the Atlantic war contained the following passage:

> *It is expected that America will now repudiate Article 2 of the Neutrality Act which forbids neutral ships to enter belligerent ports north of 30 degrees North on the eastern side of the Atlantic, and north of 35 degrees North on the western side. She is also expected to renounce her declared War Zone, and enable her ships to call at British, Irish, and Canadian ports. These steps follow naturally upon those already taken and are tantamount to direct participation in the war. The Naval Staff considers that delay in intensifying the war against merchant shipping is no longer justified, unless we are to dance to the tune of American politics.*

In November, U.S. legislation permitting American ships to use British ports became operational. But before the German naval staff could obtain Hitler's approval for retaliatory measures, the Japanese attack on Pearl Harbor occurred on December 7, and Hitler declared war on the United States on December 11. Hitler also changed his policy of avoiding war with the United States at all costs by lifting all restrictions on naval warfare on December 9. Referring to Pearl Harbor and the new naval policies in his diary on the ninth, Karl Donitz wrote:

> *This lifting of all restrictions regarding United States ships and the so called Pan-American Safety Zone has been ordered by the Fuhrer. Therefore the whole area of the American Coasts will become open for operations by U-boats, an area in which the assembly of ships takes place in single traffic at the few points of departure of Atlantic convoys. There is an opportunity here, therefore, of intercepting enemy merchant ships under conditions which have ceased almost completely for some time. Further, there will hardly be any question of an efficient patrol in the American coastal area, at least a patrol made by U-boats. Attempts must be made to utilize as quickly as possible these advantages which will disappear very shortly, and to achieve a "spectacular success" on the American Coast.*

This spectacular success would come off the coast of North Carolina.

Fregattenkapitan Gunther Hessler was chief of operations to the flag officer commanding U-boats, Admiral Karl Donitz. He once cruised twenty-two thousand miles in 135 days and sank fourteen ships, the most successful operation of the war. *Bundesarchiv, Koblenz.*

Entry by the United States into World War II created a whole new situation for the German U-boat command. More shipping than ever before had to be sunk since the American merchant marine and American shipbuilding potential would now be at the disposal of Great Britain. German U-boats would have to sink more ships than the Allies could replace. Fregattenkapitan Gunther Hessler, who was a staff officer in operations for the commander in chief of U-boats, Karl Donitz, and also his son-in-law, had already concluded in June 1941 that if the U-boats could achieve a monthly sinking rate of 800,000 tons, Great Britain could not survive. He also believed that American and British shipbuilding together could only produce about 100,000 tons of replacement shipping per month. Both of these estimates would later prove to be wishful thinking.

It's interesting to note that a very small number of men would run the upcoming operations off the North Carolina coast.

ADMIRAL KARL DONITZ

The man in charge of all U-boat operations after 1935 and Hessler's boss until the end of World War II was Admiral Karl Donitz. In 1939, he was given the title of commander in chief of U-boats (BdU). His headquarters during the period from November 1940 until March 1942 was located at Kernevel near Lorient, France, and then in Paris until March 1943. Kernevel was a large villa built by a sardine merchant on the outskirts of Lorient. The villa was close to the Atlantic, and Donitz could see his boats arriving and leaving the U-boat bunker. He would customarily send a flag signal to each boat entering and leaving the port of Lorient welcoming them back or wishing them luck on their new patrol.

During the entire span of World War II, Donitz had a small staff of only seven men. There were a few secretaries and auxiliary personnel, but only

Left: Admiral Karl Donitz. *Wolfgang Klue.*

Below: Admiral Karl Donitz inspecting the crew of a returning U-boat. *Bundesarchiv, Koblenz.*

Rear Admiral Eberhard Godt was tactical commander of U-boat operations for Admiral Karl Donitz before Gunther Hessler. *Bundesarchiv, Koblenz.*

these seven did the operational work. These men were personal friends of Donitz and former U-boat commanders. He trusted them and knew that their previous experience at sea would inspire and give confidence to his men on patrol.

His commander in chief of operations was Eberhard Godt. Godt's department was called U-boat Command, and he was virtually responsible for the movement of all operational U-boats. His first staff officer, designated A-1, was Victor Oehrn until November 1941 and then Gunther Hessler until war's end. Hessler and Godt would plan most of the operations that would take place off the North Carolina coast. The second staff officer, A-2, was Karl Daublebsky. Third was A-3 Herbert Kuppisch until June 1942 and then Johann Mohr until the end of the war. Mohr would sink forty-nine ships, seven of them off the North Carolina coast. Fourth staff officer was A-4 Hans Meckel, fifth was A-5 Werner Winter and sixth was A-6 Herbert Kuppisch after June 1942.

The British had a similar staff working to counter the U-boat operations going on under Donitz's command. The British Western Approaches Headquarters at Derby House, Liverpool, had a staff of more than one thousand to do the same job that Admiral Donitz and his seven-man staff did.

Donitz was a small man but was referred to by his men as the Lion. He was loved by all of his men and did everything he could to promote their welfare. He was also a man of habit, arising about seven o'clock in the morning and entering his U-boat situation room about nine o'clock. Each of the staff would then give their reports. Hessler, who took Oehrn's place as the A-1 in charge of operations, would brief him on the location of all U-boats and any action taken during the night. He would also report on the arrival and departures of boats operating at all of the Atlantic U-boat bases located at Lorient, Brest, Saint-Nazaire, La Pallice/La Rochelle and Bordeaux. Later on, he would meet with the returning U-boat captains and review their patrols.

U-boat pens at Lorient. *Wolfgang Klue.*

A-2 would report on the escort of U-boats by minesweepers through the minefields on approach or departure from all bases. A-3, who was the intelligence officer, would go over the movements of convoys. A-4 would review shortwave messages received from U-boats operating at sea. He would also report on longwave messages transmitted to distant submerged boats operating at a depth of up to seventy-five feet by Golieth, an enormous sending and receiving station at Calbe, Germany. Golieth was connected to Kernevel by cable. A-5 and A-6 would lastly present information about U-boat losses. It was the policy not to report personnel losses to families or the public for at least six months.

Donitz would listen to these reports for several hours each day and then try to decide what his next moves should be. He usually rested for several hours in the afternoon and, like Hitler, took a walk through the Brittany countryside with his dog, Wolf.

This he did on December 7. After the morning briefing session and during his walk that afternoon, he probably thought about the meeting he had with Hitler on September 17, 1941. After Hitler told him that all incidents with the United States were still to be avoided, he asked Donitz what the effect on U-boat operations would be if the United States were drawn into war. Donitz replied that he would like to be given a timely warning to enable him

Above: *U-505*, a captured Type IXB U-boat, is on display in Chicago. *U-boat.net.*

Right: Officers' bunks on the *U-505*. *Author's collection.*

to have his forces in position off the American coast before war was actually declared. He remembered telling Hitler that it was only in this way that full advantage could be taken of the element of surprise to strike a real blow in waters where anti-submarine defenses were still weak. Things turned out differently, however, and the German High Command was taken by surprise by the Japanese attack on Pearl Harbor. At that time, there was not a single German U-boat in American waters.

Several days later, on December 9, Donitz was informed by Naval High Command that all restrictions placed on U-boat operations against American ships or on operations in the Pan-American security zone had been removed by Hitler. In his memoirs, he recalls that on this same day, he asked Naval High Command to release twelve Type IXC U-boats for operations off the American coast. He would later be turned down.

December 11 came and went, and on that day, Hitler declared war on the United States. Great Britain breathed a sigh of relief. It would no longer have to face the Germans without full American aid.

SECURING THE SIX TYPE IXS

U-boat command's first job was to determine how many submarines were available for the upcoming offensive operations against America. The precise answer is contained in the U-Boat Command War Diary dated January 1, 1942. On this date, Germany had ninety-one operational U-boats. Of these, twenty-three were in the Mediterranean and three more under orders to proceed there. Six were stationed west of Gibraltar, and four were deployed along the Norwegian coast. Of the remaining fifty-five, thirty-three were undergoing repairs. This left only twenty-two boats at sea, and at least half of these were en route to or coming from their operational base areas. There were only eleven boats that were actively engaged in the task of sinking shipping. With respect to the heavy losses off the American coast that were to come, the historian Captain Stephen Roskill wrote, "One of the most surprising facts regarding the havoc wrought off the American coast in the early days of 1942 is that there were never more than about twelve U-boats working in these waters at any one time." Donitz would be given only six.

Expectations of Success

Even before the final plan was set, U-boat command expected great things from the first boats that would soon sail for the American coast and North Carolina. Up until now, American waters had been untouched by war. Here, most ships—including those bound for Canadian ports such as Halifax, Sidney and Nova Scotia, where the convoys were formed—sailed alone and without escort. Some form of anti-submarine defense was expected to exist but probably was not very effective. It was believed that conditions would be at least favorable for U-boat operations. U-boat command also knew that these favorable conditions would gradually disappear. When the U-boats started sinking shipping along the East Coast of the United States, the Americans would strengthen their defenses and, over time, would become more effective. Ships would not sail alone anymore, and a convoy system would be formed.

U-boat operations believed that all available forces should be used as soon as possible to take full advantage of the existing conditions before the anticipated changes occurred. U-Boat command was more correct than it realized. The anticipated changes did occur but took much longer than the Germans had anticipated.

Donitz and his operations staff recognized another advantage in their newfound freedom to venture into American waters. They knew that in the vast areas of open ocean that now constituted their operational zone, there were many focal points of shipping that could be engaged at will. Donitz relates in his memoirs: "We as the attackers could switch from one spot to another and confuse or surprise the enemy. The Americans could not provide protection for all focal points and would have to follow us around the best they could. This would cause the enemy to disperse their protective forces very effectively."

During the final week of planning the assault on America's East Coast, Godt and Donitz took a hard look at the North Carolina coast and, in particular, Cape Hatteras. Hatteras was about 3,400 miles from the Biscay U-boat pens, but traveling the distance would be worth it. They noticed from bathometric maps that the bottom here dropped off very quickly, down to six hundred feet in less than 25 miles from shore. This meant that U-boats operating here could reach deep water, easily deeper than their operating depth, in about one hour when running at 20 miles an hour on the surface. This would greatly lessen the chance of being trapped on the shallow bottom existing elsewhere.

Cape Hatteras was also the focal point of ships moving to or from the Caribbean or the Gulf Coast. The number of ships sailing singularly that would pass this point between January and July 1942, sometimes more than fifty a day, was even larger than Donitz had imagined, and the sinkings that would occur here would far exceed his estimates. His main focus would be on the tankers. He knew that if a tanker with its oil was sunk, not only would the British not get the oil they desperately needed but the ship that carried it would also be gone.

Godt, Hessler and Donitz now came up with a name for their plan of attack for the American coast. They decided to call it Operation Paukenschlag, or Drumbeat. After much bickering with the Naval High Command, they were given six Type IX boats for the mission. One of these developed an oil leak, and they ended up with five. These boats were able to carry enough fuel to reach as far as Cape Hatteras, operate several weeks and then return home without refueling.

Admiral Donitz knew what he wanted and how he would like the plan to be carried out. In his memoirs, he wrote the following a few days before his U-boats left for the American coast:

> As it was thought at U-boat Command that shipping in these areas would be found to be sailing independently, the U-boats were not massed, but were distributed over a wide area. This area I decided must not be so small that, if the enemy shipping in it were stopped or diverted, a number of U-boats would simultaneously be robbed of the chance of any action; on the other hand it must not be so big that the boats, being scattered, would not be able to threaten wide areas and would be unable to exploit to the full the opportunities it offered. Finally I was anxious to confine my first blow to an area in such a way that when we first appeared in it the enemy would be unlikely to expect us to put in an appearance soon afterwards at some other focal point. Taking these factors into consideration, I selected as the site of our first offensive against the United States the areas between the St. Lawrence River and Cape Hatteras.
>
> To ensure surprise, boats would be ordered to keep out of sight between Newfoundland and the east coast of America. In route they were to restrict their attacks to really worth-while targets—ships of 10,000 tons or over. I further stipulated that the five boats would receive from me by radio the time and date at which they could simultaneously go into action, since this depended on the weather and the time taken by the individual boats to reach the operational area.

All that was left to do was to meet with the captains of the six boats that would assault the American coast and give them their final instructions.

Donitz had planned to handpick his best and most experienced U-boat commanders for this mission. He had been assured by Hitler that there would be plenty of opportunity for this when the time came. The time, as laid out by Hitler, would have been in 1943 or later, and Donitz would have had his envisioned three-hundred-strong U-boat force in place. This didn't happen, and Donitz had no time to pick his boats or captains. He had to take what was ready to go and already located along the Biscay coast.

The Six Drumbeaters Are Chosen

He was able to secure six Type IX boats and crews that were ready to go. They were Richard Zapp in his IXC *U-66*, Reinhard Hardegen in the IXB *U-123*, Ulrich Folkers in the IXC *U-125*, Ernst Kals in the IXC *U-130*, Heinrich Bleichroft in the IXB *109* and Jurgen von Rosenstiel in the IXC *U-502*. Rosenstiel's boat developed an oil leak on the third day out and had to abort the mission and return to Lorient.

Two of these boats, *U-66* and *U-123*, would sink five ships off the North Carolina coast between January 18 and January 24.

Each of the six captains reported to U-boat headquarters at Kernevel for their instructions regarding the mission. Each would be personally briefed by Admiral Donitz. Normally Godt or Hessler would conduct the briefings, but not this time. This one was too important.

Between December 17 and December 27, all the boats were on their way. Their captains had been given basically the same orders. They were not told exactly where they were going but were told to prepare for a long cruise. The importance of sinking loaded tankers of ten thousand tons or more was stressed. They would each be given sealed operational orders by Korvettenkapitan Godt on departure. These orders were not to be opened until they crossed twenty degrees longitude. A few days later, Korvettenkapitan Mechel would send them their attack data. They were told that they would sortie independently in different operational areas. Finally, they were told that they would operate in concert, beginning offensive operations on the same day. This date would be transmitted to each captain as they approached their operational area.

U-123. Bundesarchiv, Koblenz.

Folkers in *U-125* and Rosenstiel in *U-502* left for America on December 18. Rosenstiel developed an oil leak on the twentieth and turned back on the twenty-first. Hardegen departed on the twenty-second in *U-123* and Zapp in *U-66* on Christmas Day. Kals in *U-130* and Bleinchrodt in *U-109* were the last to leave and departed on the twenty-seventh. Operation Drumbeat was underway.

THE TYPE IX U-BOAT

The boats that would carry the Drumbeat hunters to the American coast were designated as Type IXs. Two variants, IXB and IXC, were used. These U-boats were considered long-range boats able to travel as much as fifteen thousand miles without refueling. The round trip to Cape Hatteras and back from Lorient was about seven thousand miles. This would leave the boats enough fuel to operate there for two or three weeks. They could also carry up to twenty-two torpedoes, about ten more than the Type VIIs. They were 250 feet long and had a draft of just over 15 feet. Two diesel engines could push the boat along on the surface at close to twenty miles per hour, and two battery-operated electric motors could reach underwater speeds of nine

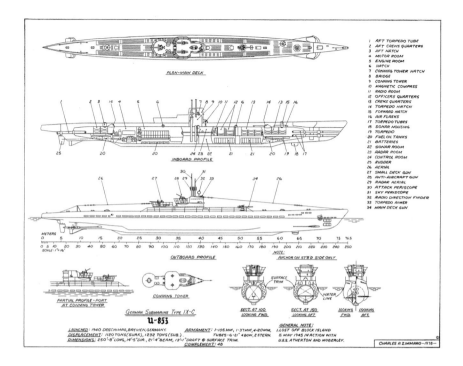

Diagram of type IX-C U-boat. *Courtesy of Charles Zimmaro.*

miles an hour. They also were armed with a 10.4-centimeter deck gun with 180 projectiles, a 3.4-centimeter antiaircraft gun and a heavy machine gun. The crews numbered four officers and forty-six men. Their major drawback was the inability to maneuver well on the surface or submerge as rapidly as the VII boats. Donitz would have preferred using Type VII boats but didn't think they were capable fuel wise of making the trip. They would be used successfully during the second wave of attackers.

CHAPTER 2

THE NORTH CAROLINA COASTLINE

Virginia Line to Cape Lookout

The majority of U-boat attacks and sinkings that occurred off the North Carolina coast between January and July 1942 took place in the offshore and inshore waters from Currituck Lighthouse in Corolla to just south of Cape Lookout. This stretch of coastline has historically been known as the Outer Banks and borders the counties of Currituck, Dare and Hyde. The following pages contain brief descriptions of each of the Banks communities as they existed during the first half of 1942. These areas are listed from north to south. This chapter is designed to help the reader visualize towns and villages along the coastline and their geographical relationship to ships sunk off their shores.

The sandy coastline of North Carolina extends from the Virginia line to the South Carolina line and stretches for more than 250 miles. The first 170 miles, all the way to Cape Lookout, are composed of a group of low, barren, sandy and nearly deserted islands known as the Outer Banks. Their shorelines, as visible from the sea, are lined with low dunes covered with sea oats. Most of the U-boat attacks and ship sinkings off the North Carolina coast would occur here. These islands are breached in a few places by narrow inlets that are constantly changing and shallow sounds that in some places are more than 30 miles in width from side to side. From Bogue Inlet southwestward, the islands almost merge with the mainland and are only separated from them by shallow, narrow waterways.

Near the center of these islands is Cape Hatteras. The Cape juts out into the Atlantic far enough to almost touch the Gulf Stream. This warm-water

Hatteras Lighthouse as it looked during the early 1940s. *History Center, Manteo, North Carolina.*

current that moves northward and can have water velocities of over five knots swings out into the Atlantic as it rounds the Cape and meets the cold-water Labrador Current. Flowing southward from the northern reaches of the Atlantic, this water mass moves inside and below the Gulf Stream and brings its cold waters to the inshore seas of the East Coast. Survivors of torpedoed ships would either find themselves in the cold, near-freezing nearshore waters or the warm Gulf Stream waters farther out. This would have a large bearing on who survived and who didn't. When these two currents meet, the turbulence that is created causes rough seas and shoaling sandbars that have historically been a trap for shipping trying to round the Cape. The shoals are called Diamond Shoals, and the area is historically referred to as the Graveyard of the Atlantic. This would be the epicenter of the majority of the upcoming U-boat attacks.

When 1942 began, there were very few people living on the beaches between the Virginia line and Cape Lookout. Most of the able-bodied men would soon leave to join the war effort, leaving the women and children to carry on. Many joined the merchant marine or worked on shipbuilding in nearby Norfolk or Newport News, Virginia.

Starting at the northern end of these islands, uninhabited white sandy shoreline backed by dunes and low vegetation extends from the Virginia line all the way to Corolla, where a lighthouse, hunting club and fewer than one hundred permanent residents lived and worked. A little farther south was the small fishing village of Duck. There were no paved roads from there to Corolla then, only a sand road established by the local residents. Fishing, crabbing, oystering and hunting were the only occupations that existed. The fifty or so residents were a tightknit bunch and didn't mind being isolated from what seemed to be the rest of the world. Names like Scarborough, Beals, Tate and Midgett were common here.

A little farther south, about six miles, Kitty Hawk, Kill Devil Hills and Nags Head formed the largest population center of the banks in the early

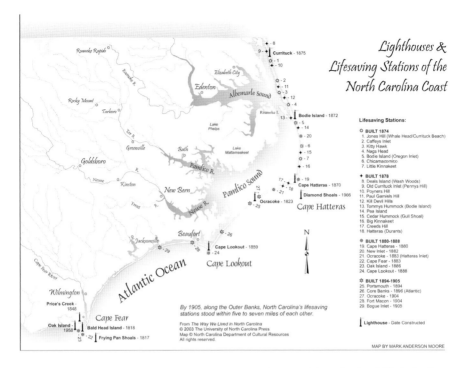

Map of lighthouses along the North Carolina coast. *Courtesy of the University of North Carolina Press. Map by Mark Anderson.*

1940s, with over one hundred full-time residents. There was a bridge to the mainland here, and some of the residents traveled to Currituck County, Elizabeth City or Virginia for work. A small summertime tourist business was also beginning to show signs of expanding, and several tourist-oriented enterprises had been started. This newfound prosperity would decrease rapidly as the war years came on. About two miles north of Oregon Inlet, the second lighthouse along the strand, the Bodie Island Lighthouse, burned every night. It, like the other lighthouses, would be a beacon for the coming U-boats.

Oregon Inlet separated the northern banks from the southern banks and Hatteras Island. The only way across the inlet was by boat. A private ferry that could carry only a few cars was also operating at this time. About thirteen miles south of the inlet on Pea Island, the small villages of Rodanthe, Waves and Salvo broke the string of sand dunes with homes that stretched for several miles. The folks who lived in these small villages depended on fishing, crabbing and wreck salvaging for their livelihood. Being completely

Diamond Shoals Lightship 69 was the first of six lightships to mark the edge of the dangerous Diamond Shoals. *Outer Banks History Center.*

isolated from the mainland, there was nothing else to do. Fewer than one hundred permanent residents were here then. Twelve miles farther south, the little village of Avon and its few fishermen were close enough to Cape Hatteras to see the lighthouse. They would also be able to see the fires from the burning ships that would soon be sunk.

The land that occupied the sharp bend in the shoreline from south to southwest and held the Cape was called Buxton. There was a coast guard station here and quite a few local residents. Thirteen miles south of Buxton, the island ended at the village of Hatteras.

A narrow, unstable inlet, Hatteras Inlet separated Hatteras Island from the nine-mile-long island of Ocracoke. At the southwestern end of this island, a small coast guard station would swell in personnel to meet the challenges of the coming U-boat war. Ocracoke Inlet provided a passageway to the sea for coast guard vessels that would go out and search for survivors from torpedoed ships. Another lighthouse here provided a beacon for both German and American vessels.

Bodie Island Lighthouse is 170 feet tall and is located on Bodie Island and the Roanoke Sound, several miles north of Oregon Inlet. *Outer Banks History Center.*

Above: During World War II, Cape Hatteras Lighthouse was located east of its present location. It is 210 feet tall, and its light can be seen from twenty miles at sea and was a beacon for U-boats during World War II. *Outer Banks History Center.*

Left: Cape Lookout Lighthouse is 163 feet tall and located near the point of Cape Lookout. *Outer Banks History Center.*

From here to Cape Lookout, only Portsmouth Island was occupied with year-round residents. Morehead City, a large population center of fishermen and boat builders, was just northwest of the Cape.

From Cape Lookout to Cape Fear, a long, wide embayment called Onslow Bay was a shallow refuge for ships moving through this area and acted as an anchorage during the first months of the war.

CHAPTER 3

JANUARY

The U-Boats Arrive off the Coast of North Carolina

The cold night of January 18, 1942, began along the coast of the Outer Banks just like other winter nights. Folks had worked all day, and most were asleep. The crews on U-boats did just the opposite, sleeping during the day while their boats rested on the bottom of the ocean and traveling on the surface and hunting for ships to sink at night.

On this night, just off the coast of Kitty Hawk and running on the surface at flank speed toward Cape Hatteras, a lone U-boat plowed along over the calm seas. The boat was the *U-123*, and its captain was Reinhard Hardegen. Hardegen, one of the five Drumbeat captains who left France the month before, had just finished sinking four ships near New York over the previous five days and was trying to reach the Cape before morning. He knew that he had only about fifty miles to go before he could continue his work by sinking more ships off the North Carolina coast.

Suddenly, at about one thirty in the morning, a large red glow followed by two booms lit up the southeastern sky. The watch officers on the bridge of *U-123* saw it and immediately notified Hardegen. What they had seen was the exploding tanker *Allen Jackson* that had just been torpedoed by *U-66*. The ship was loaded with seventy-five thousand barrels of crude oil heading for New York City and went up like a torch. Of the forty-eight crewmen on board, thirty-five would die in the fiery aftermath. The U-boat war off the coast of North Carolina had begun.

The U-boat responsible for this was *U-66*, and its captain was Richard Zapp. Zapp, another of the five Drumbeat captains, left Lorient on

Christmas Day and had proceeded directly across the Atlantic to Cape Hatteras. Arriving there on January 17, he picked a spot on the surface about seventy miles north northeast of Buxton close to Diamond Shoals and patiently waited. It was a dark night with a new moon. The seas were calm for this time of year, and the watch officers up on the bridge enjoyed the soon-to-end peace and quiet of the winter night.

THE *ALLEN JACKSON*

Off to his southwest and some forty miles away, the *Allen Jackson* was approaching the Cape. Unknown to the crew and captain, they were heading directly toward Zapp and his *U-66*.

The captain of the 430-foot-long *Jackson*, Felix Kretchmer, was aware of the fact that German U-boats could be in the vicinity but had not heard of any attacks or sinkings near Hatteras. He had timed his trip so that he would pass many miles east of the Cape and at night. He had decided, for whatever reason, that tacking was not necessary. He did, just as a precaution, black out his ship except for the red, white and green masthead lights.

The lookouts on the U-boat spotted these red and green masthead lights on the *Jackson* first, as the ship moved over the horizon about thirteen miles distant. As the *Jackson* slowly moved closer, probably still out about ten miles, more lights could be seen. The *Jackson* was not zigzagging and moving almost straight for the *U-66*.

The *Allen Jackson* was the first ship to be sunk by a U-boat off the North Carolina coast in World War II. Richard Zapp and his *U-66* sank it on the night of January 18, 1942. *The Collection of Gary Gentile.*

Fregattenkapitan Richard Zapp on the conning tower of *U-66*. *Bundesarchiv, Koblenz.*

Zapp decided to maneuver his U-boat into position for a zero-degree angle on the bow shot with his forward torpedo tubes. He would line up just to the east of the *Jackson*'s projected path and wait. It took him a while to do this, but he was finally in position. He and his first officer waited on the bridge in the darkness. The UZO, a high-powered binocular, was attached to a post on the bridge. The post, with its circular degree indicator, held the wires that ran down into the conning tower and into the attack computer. Here, as the first officer looked through the binoculars and lined up the ship for attack, data about the *Jackson*'s direction and speed would be transmitted electronically to this computer. The attack solution, including the angle for the gyro to steer and depth for the torpedoes to run, was then sent electronically to the torpedoes in the tubes.

Over three hours later, as the fully loaded, unescorted *Jackson* moved at twelve knots across the U-boat's path, Zapp, who was still on the bridge of the surfaced *U-66* with his first officer, gave the "loss" order and watched as two torpedoes sped toward the unsuspecting tanker. Both found their mark, and the resulting explosion was what Hardegen on the *U-123* saw over forty miles away. Because the *Jackson* was over seventy miles at sea, no one on Hatteras Island heard the noise or saw the explosions.

U-66 and *U-117* at sea. *Author's collection.*

As Zapp watched from 1,800 yards away, the explosions ruptured the spine of the *Jackson*, and it broke in two. Oil burned furiously as the men on the ship tried to abandon the inferno. Within thirty minutes, both halves of the ship were gone, but the sea was still blazing. Those who were able to escape the initial explosions and sinking still had to get outside the sea of burning oil to survive. The captain and twelve others made it through the night and were picked up the next morning by the destroyer *Roe*. The first ship during World War II had been sunk off the coast of North Carolina by a U-boat.

U-66 didn't hang around long after the *Jackson* went down. Zapp didn't even move in among the survivors to try to find out which ship he had sunk. He knew that his radio operators would hear it on the American emergency frequencies anyway. He also knew that dawn was coming and, with it, possibly aircraft and search boats. Zapp still wasn't sure what defensive measures were in place and what the American response might be. He turned his U-boat seaward and headed for a place farther at sea to spend the daylight hours on the bottom.

THE *LADY HAWKINS*

Late the following afternoon, he brought the *U-66* up to periscope depth and took a look around. The sea was empty and the sky was clear, so he surfaced, charged his batteries and filled the boat with fresh air. For the next six or seven hours, he headed east at 8 to 10 miles an hour looking for targets. About one o'clock in the morning of the nineteenth, his lookouts spotted a ship approaching from the north. It was a large ship and, unlike the *Jackson*, was zigzagging. It was the 420-foot *Lady Hawkins* heading from Canada to the West Indies. Loaded with passengers, the ship was blacked out and making over 15 miles an hour. Zapp considered this ship, even though it was a passenger liner, a fair target. He took chase at a full twenty knots. He was over 150 miles at sea and didn't worry about aircraft or escort vessels finding him. After an hour or so, he passed the ship and decided on a stern shot from his two aft tubes. He fired from about 3,000 feet, and both torpedoes hit their mark. The three-hundred-plus people on the ship now found themselves on a listing and sinking vessel. Lifeboats were launched, and over one hundred souls found temporary safety before the ship went down. In the end, fewer than seventy of the passengers and crew of the *Lady Hawkins* were finally rescued by the SS *Coamo* four days later.

Two ships had now been sunk off Hatteras in less than two days. Mainlanders still had not seen the explosions or heard the torpedo blasts because of the distance at sea where both sinkings occurred. On the nineteenth, this would change.

Reinhard Hardegen and *U-123* were close to the beach near Oregon Inlet and moving southward toward Cape Hatteras. He had no intention of turning back northward. He had seen the orange glow of the *Andrew Jackson* burning and anticipated sinking a ship or two himself before dawn.

Watching the lights along the beach and the intermittent flashes from the Bodie Island Lighthouse less than five miles away, a small ship was seen by *U-123*'s lookouts passing between the U-boat and the shore and moving toward the north. Hardegen decided to sink it and gave chase. The first torpedo fired after about a thirty-minute chase ran off course, and another one was fired after pursuing the ship for several more miles. Although the ship was identified as the 4,500-ton freighter *Brazos*, its identity was never confirmed. The sinking was close enough to the beach at Kitty Hawk that the noise of the torpedo striking the ship could have been heard by people living there. No record of this was ever made.

According to Hardegen's KTB, he immediately turned south again and proceeded close inshore in very shallow water toward Cape Hatteras. He had used two of his five remaining torpedoes on the phantom *Brazos*.

CITY OF ATLANTA

It wasn't long before more ships were sighted moving both north and south. The next one Hardegen picked was the five-thousand-ton former passenger liner *City of Atlanta*. The ship was heading south at ten miles an hour and carrying freight, not passengers. It had just passed by Wimble Shoals Buoy and Salvo when the bridge watch spotted it. Hardegen was able to pass the ship and set up for a perfect shot from his forward torpedo tubes. One torpedo was all it took. At about two o'clock in the morning, the violent blast caused the ship to sink almost immediately and killed all but three of its forty-eight-man crew.

Eight miles west in Avon, residents were awakened by the blast, fire and concussion that followed. Gib Gray recounted how he was awakened with the rest of his family by the exploding torpedoes. Rushing around his home to see what had happened, he finally looked toward the sea and saw the burning ship. He said:

> *I was scared to death and didn't know what was going to happen next. I had heard my parents talking about the Germans and the U-boats but didn't pay much attention to it. I had no idea what a U-boat was or what it could do. Now it all became real and this was just the beginning. It was about three o'clock in the morning now and I didn't go back to sleep at all. I heard more racket during the next few hours that must have been the* Ciltvaira *and the* Malay *being hit. I thought about going over to the beach the next day and looking around to see if I could find anything but don't remember doing it.*

Billy Baum, a legendary charter boat captain who still lives in Wanchese, remembers that the blast blew the chimneys off and the windows out of several of his friends' homes in Avon. Baum recalls, "We thought the ship must have been loaded with dynamite. This didn't slow any of us down though. We still went fishing every day we could just like we always did."

Hardegen finally was at the Cape. He had two torpedoes and several hours of darkness left before sunrise. He was also running low on fuel. He intended to finish his job before dawn and head back to France.

THE *MALAY*

As he watched the *City of Atlanta* burn, another ship passed east of his position heading south. It was the 470-foot tanker *Malay*. He didn't want to waste his two torpedoes on what he thought was a small ship. Although he underestimated the size of the *Malay*, which was over eight thousand tons, he decided to sink it with his 10.5-cm deck gun and save the torpedoes for larger game. He had in his magazine over two hundred shells for the gun— more than enough. The projectile from the shell was powerful enough to sink a ship with a single hit and could travel up to ten miles. He could have easily shelled the shore and Avon, which would have scared the residents to death if that was part of his mission, but it was not.

Leaving the *City*'s crew, who were still floundering around in the sea, he gave chase and soon ran down the *Malay*. The gun crew fired at least five shells into the ship, setting it on fire. This proved to be not enough to sink it, and Hardegen would return to try to finish the job later. *U-123* still had its two torpedoes, and another ship would go down before dawn. *U-123* turned northeast and moved slowly away.

THE *CILTVAIRA*

The 3,800-hundred-ton Latvian freighter *Ciltvaira* would be next. The ship, with a crew of thirty-two, was about ten miles east of Avon and heading south at nine miles an hour. The *U-123*'s lookouts spotted it, and within minutes, one torpedo slammed into the port side of the engine room. Most of the crew were able to abandon ship and were picked up shortly afterward. The ship remained afloat for days, and the spot of its sinking was never positively found.

Hardegen had one torpedo left, and he decided to spend it on the *Malay*. *U-123* turned southwest, caught up with the ship in about an hour and fired its last torpedo. The *Malay* was hit in an empty compartment, but this was not enough to sink it, and the ship made it back to Hampton Roads the following day.

U-123 turned east on January 19 and was on its way back to Lorient. Hardegen had two confirmed sinkings off the North Carolina coast and possibly another in the unconfirmed *Brazos*. He had also made the residents of Dare County absolutely certain that the U-boats were off the coast and more death and destruction were certain to follow.

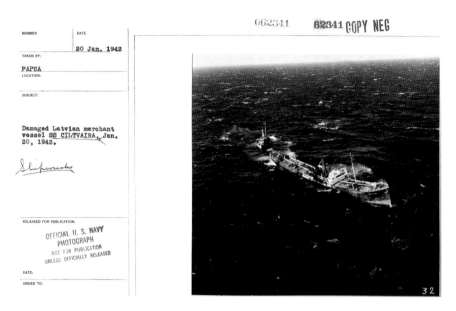

NUMBER

DATE
20 Jan, 1942

TAKEN BY:
PAPUA

LOCATION:

SUBJECT:

Damaged Latvian merchant
vessel SS CILTVAIRA, Jan.
20, 1942.

RELEASED FOR PUBLICATION:

OFFICIAL U. S. NAVY
PHOTOGRAPH
NOT FOR PUBLICATION
UNLESS OFFICIALLY RELEASED

DATE:

ISSUED TO:

Ciltvaira, sunk east of Avon by *U-123*. *Author's collection.*

The *Norvana-York*

Richard Zapp and his *U-66* were still around. He had moved northwest since sinking the *Lady Hawkins* and was surfaced off Kitty Hawk the night of the twentieth when he spotted a ship heading north about twelve miles off the coast. It was the three-thousand-ton freighter *Norvana*. The ship, 230 feet long and previously known as the *York*, was heading for Philadelphia with a crew of thirty men. Zapp used his stern torpedo tubes to send the *Norvana* to the sandy 100-foot bottom. None of the crew survived.

York, renamed *Norvana*, sunk off Kitty Hawk by *U-66*. *National Archives.*

THE *VENORE*

Zapp decided to move back south and wait near the Cape for more ships. On the night of the twenty-third, he was on the surface about eighty miles east of Hatteras, just east of the shoals, and waiting. Just to the southwest of him, two ships were moving toward him in the darkness. The freighter *Venore*, loaded with iron ore, was leading the way, followed by the tanker *Empire Gym*. The *Gym* was making better speed than the *Venore* and was overtaking it. As both ships neared *U-66*'s position, the *Gym* passed the *Venore* and made a sharp turn to the north. Zapp fired first at the *Gym* and hit it amidships. The terrific explosion that followed sank the ship immediately. Two more torpedoes were fired at the closely following *Venore*. It took one more torpedo, Zapp's last, to sink the final ship *U-66* would claim in January. Zapp, like Hardegen, was sailing for France. Their visit to America was over for now. They had sunk seven ships off the Outer Banks and would be treated as heroes when they arrived home.

January also ended for the folks living along the coast of North Carolina. From Duck to Buxton, the reality of war had arrived and would last for many months to come. Pristine beaches from Corolla to Cape Lookout were covered with tar created by the floating oil spilled from burning tankers and freighters. Debris of all kinds, including the bodies of dead crewmen, washed ashore, too. Residents who had always left their doors unlocked locked them now and began to wonder if an invasion might be next. They also wondered what the military response would be and how long they would have to wait before it started.

CHAPTER 4

THE NAVY MAKES CHANGES

The navy's designation in January 1942 for the area off the coast of North Carolina's Outer Banks was the Eastern Sea Frontier. This stretch of ocean and coastline extended from the Canadian border to North Carolina and two hundred miles out to sea. The man responsible for defensive operations here was Admiral Adolphus Andrews. He had no ships under his command and would need to ask for help from the commander of the U.S. fleet in the event of an attack from the sea or air. His headquarters was in the federal building in downtown Manhattan. His boss was Admiral Earnest King, commander in chief of the U.S. Naval Fleet. King had all of the navy's ships and the coast guard under his command and was not, in January 1942, ready to release any of them to Andrews to defend the Eastern Sea Frontier. He was busy sending destroyer escorts to accompany troop convoys making their way across the Atlantic and was holding most of his online destroyers in reserve. Of the twenty-one destroyers available at that time, King would only release two or three for anti-submarine warfare (ASW) duty on the eastern seaboard. When Andrews asked for help after the January U-boat attacks, King hedged. He knew that Germany had the *Tripitz*, a pocket battleship, ready to move into the Atlantic and attack his convoys, and he wanted to have the ships ready to meet this threat if necessary. Andrews, for the time being, was on his own. He did, however, manage to put together a small defensive force of twenty small, old vessels to start the job. He had seven coast guard cutters, seven sub chasers, two gunboats and four yachts. At the time, he had no aircraft under his direct command.

It's interesting to note that at this time all land-based aircraft were under the control of the army air corps. The only aircraft controlled by the navy were carrier-based planes, Catalinas, small scout planes and blimps. In January, King attempted to get control of the land-based aircraft for ASW patrols but was turned down. The desire for control of military aviation had already developed into a hot dispute between the army and the navy, and even the sinking of several ships by U-boats was not enough to break the existing arrangement.

Several events occurred that led to an improvement in this situation. First, General Arnold Krogstad, who had over ninety large aircraft at airfields along the East Coast under his command, was assigned the duty of commander of air anti-submarine

Admiral Earnest King, commander in chief of the U.S. fleet and chief of naval operations. King was the only person to hold both of these jobs at the same time. *U.S. Navy.*

warfare for the entire East Coast. Second, he moved his headquarters to the federal building in Manhattan. His office was just down the hall from Admiral Andrews. The two men got together and formed a working relationship that worked well and didn't formally violate the army-navy dispute over control of coastal air forces. The major problem was that neither Andrews nor Krogstad knew how to find and sink U-boats, and their initial attempts didn't work too well. They would slowly improve in the future.

When Reinhard Hardegen in his *U-123* started sinking ships in the Eastern Sea Frontier, Andrews and Krogstad sent their planes, blimps and ships out to try to sink the U-boats responsible. This well-intended attempt would prove futile for three more months.

It wasn't long after the initial sinkings off North Carolina that the folks living along the coast began asking one another where the navy was. The Navy Department was quick to respond that several U-boats had been sunk and that the details about the actions were being kept secret for security reasons. This was untrue; in fact, the navy-army team had not made a

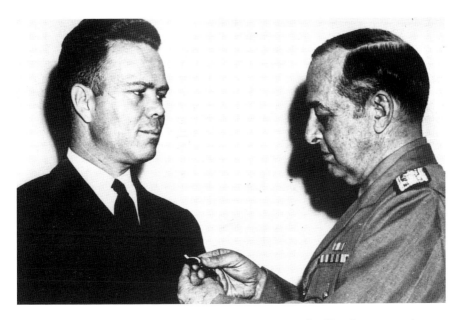

Vice Admiral Adolphus Andrews, commander of the Eastern Sea Frontier, presents the Navy Cross to Lieutenant Commander Hamilton Howe for sinking the *U-85*. *Bill Hughes.*

single effective attack against the January U-boats. Even though the Navy Department claimed that many boats had been sunk or captured, none of the three boats operating off the North Carolina and East Coast during January had been hit.

As January drew to a close, an event that happened on the twenty-eighth completely changed the navy's "secrecy" policy. A navy pilot, Donald Mason, dropped several bombs on what he thought was a U-boat. When the Navy Department got wind of this, it was decided that letting the public know would be a great propaganda tool. A message was even crafted that supposedly was sent by Mason after he dropped the bombs from his PBY-Catalina. The message read, "Sighted sub, sank same."

Donitz, at his headquarters back in France, had good reason to pronounce the foray of U-boats into North Atlantic waters a great success. The U.S. Navy had not done much to stop him in January.

CHAPTER 5

BLACKOUT

February Begins with the Loss of Naval Enigma

THE SCHLUSSEL M4 ENIGMA MACHINE

During World War II, the German military used an electro-mechanical cipher machine called Enigma to encode plain text messages in secret form. The one used by the German navy, the Schlussel M4 Naval Enigma with four rotors, was on all German U-boats after mid-January 1942, and the code was not broken until the following December. The machine was so good that the number of ways a single letter could be encoded theoretically was 3x10 to the 114th power. Not until 1974, when F.W. Winterbotham's book *The Ultra Secret* revealed that the Allies had read Enigma ciphers throughout the war, did the Germans admit that their Enigma machine had been compromised in World War II.

The cipher machine that had been in service before the M4 was the M3 and used three rotors. A rotor was a wheel with twenty-six contacts on each side. Each contact represented a letter of the alphabet. Wires ran between each contact to a different contact on the other side so that a letter entering one side would come out another on the other side. This letter would then move on electronically to the next rotor. The more rotors, the more complicated it became to solve the cipher. The British codebreakers at Bletchley Park had been reading the messages from this machine for quite some time and were supplying the information to the United States government. This information included the movements and locations of all

M4 Schlussel M Enigma machine recovered from the radio room of the *U-85*. *Author's collection.*

U-boats and was shared with the Navy Department. The new machine with four rotors on the U-boat net triton resulted in the blocking of all encoded messages sent and received from U-boats operating along the American coast in February 1942. The consequences of this loss that would fall on the U-boat battles of the North Carolina coast were many. Information that was contained in the messages sent on the new machine created the following shortfalls for the Allies:

- The U-boats would concentrate their attacks off Cape Hatteras due to the proximity to deep and safer water. If this had been known, the navy would have beefed up its ASW forces in this area.
- U-boats were to operate alone rather than in wolf packs and observe radio silence. If this had been known, convoying might have been started sooner. It had already been shown by the

A I A	Ungefähr	H O A	Unmöglichkeit *von*
F A Q	Ungehorsam *von (Hauptwort)*	H O B	Wegen/Infolge der Unmöglichkeit *von*
H P J	Ungelegen *für/zu*	P P T	Unnötig *für/zu/um zu*
H P I	Ungelegenheit(en)	F A U	Unordentlich
H O O	Ungenau	F A T	Unordnung
H U J	Ungenügend	K F V	In Unordnung
H U K	Ungenügend *für/zu/um zu*	P Q U	Unpassend *für/zu*
B Q K	Ungeschickt	H N Q	Unpassierbar
K E E	Ungeschützt gegen (i. S. v. offen gegen)	V I V	Unpraktisch
H N I	Ungesetzlich	V V J	Unrecht
P O X	Ungesund	W A F	Hab/Hat/Haben unrecht
P N D	Ungewiß *über*	W A G	Hatte(n) unrecht
P N H	Ungewöhnlich	H W Z	Unregelmäßig
V T Q	Ungleich	H X A	Unregelmäßigkeit(en)
E X V	Unglücksfall (-fälle)	H P K	Unrichtig
A J E	Leichter Unglücksfall *an/in*		Uns
A J A	{ Unglücksfall ist eingetreten *an/in* / Unglücksfall stieß zu *in*	V W M	Zu uns (3. Fall)
A J D	Schwerer Unglücksfall *an/in*	V W N	Uns selbst (4. Fall)
A J B	Ursache(n) des Unglücksfalls	K K A	Unser(e, en) (1. u. 4. Fall)
P O T	{ Unglücklich / Unglücklicherweise	H T J	Unschuldig *an*
W A J	Ungültig	W A P	Unsicher (wegen Gefährdung)
P O O	Ungünstig *für/um zu/zu*	C Y	Es ist unsicher, auf dem Ankerplatz zu bleiben
P Q V	Unhaltbar		
E X X	Unheilvoll	P N D	Unsicher *über* (i. S. v. zweifelhaft oder ungewiß)
P P B	Uniform(en) *von*		Unsicherheit
G M B	Unklar (i. S. v. nicht benutzbar)	P N E	Wegen Unsicherheit *von*
G L Y	Unklar von (i. S. v. vertörnt)	H W N	Unsichtbar
G L Z	Unklar kommen von	P O Q	Untauglich *für/zu*
G M A	Bin... unklar gekommen von	P O R	Untauglichkeit
A Y E	Sie werden unklar kommen von meinem Anker	C I S	Unten auf (i. S. v. am Boden) / Unten in
G M B	Unklar machen	V W G	Unter
G M C	Hab... unklar gemacht	A W S	Unter (i. S. v. dazwischen)
H B X	Meine Schraube ist unklar durch Trosse	P N M	Unter keinem (-r, -n) (z. B. unter keinen Bedingungen)
V U P	Unkosten *von*	O I V	Unter-
D C K	Bestehen/Gibt es irgendwelche Unkosten	H V W	Unterbrechen
D C L	Wie hoch sind die Unkosten	H V X	Hab.../Ist... unterbrochen
D C I	Unkosten sind mäßig	H V Y	Werde(n, Wird) unterbrochen
D C J	Sind die Unkosten mäßig	E Z E	Unterbrochen (i. techn. S.)
H N H	Unkundig *von*	H V P	Unterbrochen (v. Feuern)
P M R	Bin, Ist (Sind) unkundig	X	Unterbrechen Sie Ihr gegenwärtiges Vorhaben, und warten Sie auf meine Signale
P P Y	Unlesbar		
R I Q	Unmittelbar		
A P P	Unmittelbar nach/danach	H V Z	Unterbrechung(en)
B X G	Unmittelbar vor/bevor	A J G	Unterbringen
H O C	Unmöglich *für/zu*	A J J	Hab... untergebracht
H O D	Unmöglich infolge von/wegen	A J K	Werde(n, Wird) unterbringen
H O E	Es ist unmöglich *für/zu*	A I N	Unterbringung wird benötigt *für/in*

An Enigma code page recovered from the radio room of the *U-85*. *Author's collection.*

British that only one or two ships out of a convoy would be sunk before the escorts could find and drive the U-boat down or sink it.

- Admiral King was holding back many of his destroyers for troop convoy escorts. Enigma traffic revealed that the large German surface ships were unable to venture out into the Atlantic at this time and attack convoys in the North Atlantic. If this had been known through Enigma information, King would have been free to release these destroyers for ASW duty along the East Coast and particularly the Cape Hatteras area.

- The Drumbeat attack was an all-out offensive against East Coast shipping. Every U-boat that was available to Donitz was sent here starting in December 1942. It also turned out that over the first six months of that year, the number of ships sunk along the East Coast of the United States was much greater than the number of ships sunk in North Atlantic convoys. If the fact had been known that almost all of the U-boats would be operating along the East Coast rather than in the convoy lanes, a greater number of destroyers for ASW duty could have been assigned to the East Coast and particularly the Hatteras area.

- The plan by the Germans to send large U-vessels capable of refueling and resupplying U-boats operating along the East Coast was already in the works and would start in April 1942. If this had been known, countermeasures could have been developed to sink these "milch cows" and any U-boats that were surfaced taking on supplies around them.

Enigma machine (*far left*) in the radio room of an unidentified U-boat. *National Archives.*

Left: Enigma machine rotors recovered from the *U-85*. Note that the wheel numbers and the machine number, 2946, appear on each wheel. *Roy Parker.*

Right: Enigma machine rotors. *Roy Parker.*

In other words, if M4 decrypts had been available to the navy from February on, the number of ships sunk, lives lost and cargos destroyed off the North Carolina coast could have been reduced.

MORE SHIPS GO TO THE BOTTOM OFF THE NORTH CAROLINA COAST IN FEBRUARY

Donitz was able to send twenty-six U-boats to American waters in January. Twelve of these were type IXs, and fourteen were type VIIs. Four of the IXB boats were to patrol the sea frontier between New York and Hatteras. Several Type VIIs were also ordered to venture as far as Cape Hatteras. When these boats reached their patrol areas in early February, they were surprised to find that anti-submarine defenses had not increased and were almost nonexistent. By February 8, however, Admiral King had released eight Atlantic Fleet destroyers to Admiral Andrews for his use in the Eastern Sea Frontier. It would turn out that by the middle of the month, all of these had to be recalled for North Atlantic convoy duty except the *Roe*. To help fill this gap, King released four old World War I "four stackers." These destroyers included the *Dickerson* and the *Jacob Jones*.

Admiral King also asked Andrews to submit a convoy plan to protect East Coast shipping. Andrews believed that a much larger number of ships would be required to adequately protect the large number of vessels passing through the frontier each day and recommended that until a suitable number of escort ships could be provided, no convoy system should be initiated.

THE *AMERIKALAND*

Five ships would go down as a result of U-boat attacks off the North Carolina coast in February. The month began with the sinking of one of the largest and fastest freighters in the world twenty miles south of the Virginia line and off Wash Woods.

The 15,400-ton fully lighted Swedish ship *Amerikaland* was proceeding south at close to twenty miles an hour when two torpedoes struck it. The Type IXB *U-106*, captained by Herman Rasch, had been waiting on the surface and, after firing its torpedoes, watched the ship go down almost immediately. Rasch had left France on January 3 with the second wave of Paukenslag boats and would not return home until February 22. He would sink five ships during his stay along the East Coast.

Several lifeboats were launched, with the captain of the *Amerikaland* and twelve sailors in one and twenty-seven men in two others. Captain Schutz and the crewmen in his lifeboat were rescued two days later by a passing freighter, but the other two boats were never seen or heard from again. The month had thus started with the ASW situation just about as bad as it had been the previous month and not expected to improve much in the immediate future.

THE *VICTOLITE*

The next ship to go down was the 11,500-ton Canadian tanker *Victolite* on February 11. The U-boat captain that sank her was Teddy Suhren in the *U-564*. He left France with the second wave of boats on January 18 and would not return until March 3. Suhren would sink thirty-three ships during the war.

The tanker, moving north at night just east of Caffey's Inlet, went down after being hit by both torpedoes and deck gun fire. Suhren commented later that this juicy morsel was blown sky high.

It's interesting to note that the *U-564* was a Type VIIC. Until now, this type class was not considered capable of making the long trip to the East Coast of the United States without refueling. The boat was 220 feet long, carried a maximum of fourteen torpedoes and had a range of about nine thousand miles. The type IX boats that had been used up until now were 252 feet long and could carry twenty-two torpedoes. They had a range of up to sixteen thousand miles. After several of the Type VII boats had ventured down from Canadian waters in January, Donitz was convinced that the VIIs could operate along the East Coast for several weeks if they followed the Great Circle route over and conserved as much fuel as possible. This proved to be true over the following months.

Suhren would later state, "I first crossed the pond with the second wave. The leading engineer had filled every available crevice with diesel oil. Traveling at our most economical speed so as to use as little fuel as possible we finally made it up to Cape Hatteras where we were convinced that the shipping was just waiting for us."

THE *BLINK*

The Norwegian freighter *Blink* would be next. Moving south on the night of February 11 about 150 miles east of Cape Hatteras, the ship was met by Korvettenkapitan Klaus Scholtz, who was moving north in his IXB *U-108*. After finally sinking the *Blink* with three torpedoes, Scholtz moved in to take a closer look. Of the thirty-one men on the freighter, only six would survive after a harrowing six days on the open sea.

THE *BUARQUE*

The *Buarque* was a five-thousand-ton Brazilian tramp freighter that carried both freight and passengers. On the night of February 15, about twenty miles east of Corolla, the ship was proceeding northward to New York with freight, a crew of seventy-four men and eleven passengers. Since the vessel was from a neutral country and was flying a large illuminated Brazilian flag, its captain, Joao Joaquim de Moura, saw no need to darken his ship and steamed along at twelve miles an hour with all lights glaring. Earlier in the day off Pea Island, he had been followed by a U-boat and not attacked. The boat passed him in broad daylight heading north. De Moura assumed from this that he was home free as far as having trouble with the U-boats. This false sense of security would not last much longer.

Getting his boat in position for a portside attack, Heinz-Otto Schultze maneuvered past the slow-moving freighter and waited on the surface. He had plenty of time for his first watch officer to attach the UZO on the bridge and send the needed information to the attack computer. He had arrived off the Hatteras area on February 14 in the Type VIIC *U-432* and was patroling northward to the Maryland coast. He undoubtedly was able to see the large illuminated Brazilian flag flying from the fantail and the one painted on the side of the hull.

For whatever reason, Schultze decided to sink the freighter no matter what. He fired one torpedo into the port side of the *Buarque*. It was midnight, and almost everyone on the *Buarque* was asleep. After a terrific explosion, all on board frantically tried to reach the lifeboats, and eventually, five were lowered. Just a short time later, about twenty minutes after the torpedo struck, the ship went down bow first.

The *Buarque* sinking off Corolla. *National Archives.*

It was a rough night, with a heavy ground swell rolling in from the northeast. The water was almost at the freezing point, and the wind was howling. Although everyone got off, the four lifeboats soon became separated. Being some twenty miles from land and at night, the chance of rescue seemed small.

Fortunately, the radio operator on the *Buarque* had time to send out a position report with an SOS. About seven o'clock in the morning, a plane spotted one of the lifeboats and radioed its position. Shortly thereafter, with the help of additional aircraft, the second lifeboat was spotted. Late that afternoon, the survivors from both lifeboats were picked up by the coast guard cutter *Calypso*.

It took almost two more days to locate the other lifeboats. On February 17, the tanker *Eagle* rescued twenty-seven from one boat and the destroyer *Jacob Jones* picked up sixteen from the other. Most were suffering from frostbite and shock but survived.

If sinking one neutral ship was not bad enough for Schultze, his next victim was the Brazilian-registered four-thousand-ton *Olinda*. The Brazilian government immediately froze German assets in Brazil and issued a strong protest to the German government in Berlin. The Germans sent an apology, but nothing more came of the incident. Finally, after more of its ships were sunk, Brazil declared war on Germany.

As for Kapitanleutnant Schultze, he continued his patrol to the Maryland coast and back to Hatteras and, in the process, sank six confirmed ships. This was the best patrol of a Type VIIC U-boat to date.

THE *NORLAVORE*

Like so many ships during World War II, the 2,700-ton freighter *Norlavore* left Venezuela on February 22 bound for New York and never was heard from again. No German U-boat ever took responsibility for its sinking. Radio logs do indicate that the ship was probably sunk on February 24 somewhere off the coast of Cape Hatteras. One U-boat was in the vicinity at the time but did not take credit for sending the *Norlavore* to the bottom. This was Kapitanleutnant Schultze's *U-432*. He would use his last torpedo and deck gun to sink one more ship off the North Carolina coast before returning to France. It would be the *Marore*.

The *Marore*

The 550-foot, 8,200-ton ore carrier *Marore* would be the longest ship sunk off the North Carolina coast during World War II. The ship, with a crew of thirty-nine captained by Charles E. Nash, left Chile in early February and was heading for Baltimore, Maryland, with 23,000 tons of iron ore. Because of the heavy load, it could make no more than ten knots.

The trip up the west coast of South America and through the Panama Canal was uneventful. Passing into the Atlantic and up the East Coast, Captain Nash decided to travel blacked out at night. Moving past Cape Hatteras and Diamond Shoals on the night of the twenty-sixth, he would be off Rodanthe and Wimble Shoals by midnight.

Waiting for him there on the surface, Kapitanleutnant Schultze and his *U-432* lined up for the attack. He had expended all of his fourteen torpedoes except one and decided to use it on the *Marore*.

Just after midnight, with most of the crew sleeping, a lone torpedo struck the starboard side of the *Marore* about one hundred feet behind the bow. The explosion aroused the sleeping crew, who began to scamper for their assigned lifeboats. The captain immediately ordered "abandon ship," and all got off in three lifeboats.

Marore, the longest ship to be sunk off the North Carolina coast during World War II, was torpedoed by *U-432*. *National Archives.*

As Schultze watched the burning ore carrier, he realized that it probably wouldn't sink without additional damage. He had used his last torpedo and ordered his gun crew to man the 88mm deck cannon and fire away. Eventually, as the men in the lifeboats watched, the *Marore* was continually shelled by the powerful 88. The ship went down stern first less than thirty minutes later. Schultze, happy with his work and entire trip, set sail for France.

All three lifeboats began to row toward land twelve miles away. About nine hours later, two of the boats were spotted by the tanker *John D. Gill* and the twenty-five men in them picked up. The other boat with Captain Nash and thirteen crew members was spotted by lookouts at the Big Kinnakeet Coast Guard Station, and a launch was sent out to pick them up. They all were reunited in Norfolk, Virginia.

The *Marore* would be the last ship sunk off the North Carolina coast in February. March would be very different in the number of sinkings and the casualties that resulted.

One other ship was sunk by a German U-boat during the closing days of February. It was not off the North Carolina coast, but the significance of its sinking would directly affect the war effort there. It was the destroyer *Jacob Jones*.

On the afternoon of February 22, two of the four-stack destroyers on loan to the Eastern Sea Frontier for anti-submarine duty left New York for an ASW patrol. They were the *Dickerson* and the *Jacob Jones*. By five o'clock the next morning, the *Jones* was off the Delaware Capes heading south at about fifteen miles an hour. It was still dark, but a full moon shined brightly on the calm sea. The destroyer, commanded by Lieutenant Commander Hugh Black, was not zigzagging or making any evasive maneuvers. Up ahead and on the surface, the Type VII *U-578* waited. Its commander, Ernst-August Rehwinkel, had been in the first of eleven boats that had left France in mid-February to arrive in United States waters. As the *Jones* passed in front of him, he fired two torpedoes from his bow tubes in rapid succession. Both hit the *Jones* with enough explosive force to blow the ship apart. Many of the 190-man crew were killed immediately. Others, clinging to debris in the water, died when all of the destroyer's depth charges exploded as it sank. Captain Black had ordered them all armed for immediate action if a U-boat were spotted. Only 11 survived and were picked up several hours later by a small coast guard patrol boat. This was the second U.S. destroyer sunk by a U-boat since October 31, 1941. In spite of claims by the Navy Department indicating otherwise, no U-boats had yet been sunk in American waters.

CHAPTER 6

PROTECTING THE HOMELAND

When March began, much had changed along the Outer Banks of North Carolina. The pristine, sandy beaches were covered with oil, debris and bodies from the sunken ships. Residents of the coastal villages locked their doors for the first time in fear that Germans were landing or would land on the beaches. Unfamiliar faces seen by bankers were looked upon as German spies. Folks even began to suspect citizens in their communities of being collaborators. The growing summer tourist trade would not happen that year and possibly not for many years to come. Men were leaving their families to join the military or work in defense plants or shipyards in distant places. Coast guard stations that had been deactivated were being reactivated, and guardsmen were patrolling the beaches. For those left who made their living fishing in the ocean, new rules made it all but impossible to continue their work. Night fishing was prohibited and ocean fishing greatly restricted. It was a time of change and deep uncertainty about what the future held.

An increased presence of the military was also evident to the bankers. First to come were mobile defense forces sent by the army. These men and women, some twenty-five thousand strong, were deployed all along the 375 miles of North Carolina's coastline. Artillery batteries were set up to meet any invading force that might try to land. A Coastal Defense Warning Service was also initiated that would recruit civilians to act as coast watchers to be on the lookout for any suspicious activity that might indicate that a person or persons was trying to disrupt the war effort. War emergency ordinances were being formulated to give police powers to air raid wardens and other civilian volunteers. Blackouts were ordered, but it would be another month before coastal businesses would fully observe them. The 111th National Guard Infantry Regiment sent a unit to Kitty Hawk to set up a radar station near Kitty Hawk Village. A watch tower was also built here on a high sand hill to enable spotters to see far out in the ocean and observe any enemy movements that might occur.

Coast guard stations that had been closed were opened. Jeep and foot patrols and later horse patrols by an ever-increasing number of new military recruits would cover the seven-mile gaps between these stations for the rest of the war years. The navy also sent men to reinforce the coast guard and help patrol the beaches. Local residents provided a place to stay for many of these soldiers as the islands swelled to over twice their normal population.

Two other proposals that would come into full play in several months are worth mentioning here. The first was the creation of a civilian "Hooligan Navy." It would officially be known as the U.S. Coast Guard Corsair Fleet. This "Navy" would be made up of private yachts, fishing craft, sailboats and any other craft that was capable of patrolling the nearshore ocean waters and reporting any U-boat activity that might be observed. This idea was first suggested to the Navy Department in June 1941 when the owner of a swordfishing fleet offered to carry out patrols and conduct observations of the ocean waters where his boats fished if the navy would install radio-telephone equipment on his fleet. The idea was turned down.

Several months later, another plan was put forth by the Cruising Club of America, which offered the navy use of over fifty large sailing vessels with trained crews to patrol the waters off the East Coast and watch for U-boats. The idea seemed like a good one but was initially again turned down by the navy.

After the disastrous months of January and February, the offer was made again. Realizing that the public was mad and wanted action, Admiral King looked more favorably at the proposal but still hesitated to go forward with it. This did not deter the Cruising Club of America. It worked throughout the month of March, lining up vessels to offer the navy. The plan was finally accepted in May, and Admiral King turned over responsibility for its implementation to the coast guard reserve.

In the beginning, the folks volunteering to serve were as diverse as the vessels that were put into service. Beach boys, college dropouts, fishermen, surfers, would-be sailors and others applied and were usually accepted. Thus, the name "Hooligan Navy" came into being. It was even reported later that after some of the craft were allowed to carry depth charges, a call came in from one of the Hooligan craft stating that the crew on the boat had "sighted a sub and sank self." The boat wasn't fast enough to get out of the way of the exploding depth charge. Several of these craft were docked at the Ocracoke Coast Guard Station during the war and were used for patrols and rescues of survivors of ships sunk off the North Carolina coast.

The other innovation was the formation of the Civil Air Patrol on December 1, 1941. An offer was made by this group to use their own planes to patrol the coastal waters of the Eastern Sea Frontier and search for U-boats, survivors of torpedoed ships and ships that had been attacked but not sunk. The idea seemed good to the navy and resulted in President Roosevelt ordering the Navy Department to make use of the civilian pilots immediately.

Planes began flying patrols along the Eastern Sea Frontier in March, but their use off the North Carolina coast didn't begin until July. By that time, two coastal patrol groups had been created, one stationed in Manteo and the other in Beaufort. The one in Manteo was commanded by Alan Watkins and given the designation Patrol Squadron 16. This squadron operated from a hastily built runway at Skyco, a marshy wooded area just south of Manteo and near the center of Roanoke Island. Operations from this location were extremely hazardous, and the squadron was moved to Manteo Airport the following year. The Beaufort runway was completed in August and opened in September.

The squadrons had twelve single-engine planes each that carried the pilot and an observer. They were not armed. Two planes always flew together. If one went down, the other could circle until hopefully help arrived. The only instruments the planes had were a compass and a radio to contact their base. They flew out as far as fifty miles, usually at low altitude.

Although the situation seemed very bad when February ended and March began, it would get much worse. Over twenty-five ships would go down off the Carolina coast in March, more than any other month of the war.

Chapter 7

A Bloody March

March began with the destroyer situation no better than it was in February when there were no more than five destroyers per day on ASW duty in the Eastern Sea Frontier. Land-based aircraft had started to make regular patrols but had not been successful in sinking a U-boat.

During the month of March, King would provide fourteen different destroyers for Andrews to use temporarily in defending the Eastern Sea Frontier. There were, however, only two destroyers in use per day during the whole month. One of these was the USS *Roper* (DD147).

Donitz, back in France and pleased with results of the American campaign so far, sent eighteen more U-boats to American waters in February. Only thirteen of these actually got there. They would arrive along the East Coast all during the month of March. Eight of these boats would spend most of their time off the North Carolina coast and sink over twenty ships before returning home. The boats, captains and ships they sent to the bottom were as follows:

Johann Mohr, Type IXB *U-124*: *British Resource, E.M. Clark, Papoose, Ceiba, Kassandra Loulaudis, Naeco* and *E.H. Hutton*
Georg Lassen, Type IXC *U-160*: *City of New York* and *Equipoise*
Erwin Rostin, Type IXC *U-158*: *John D. Gill, Ario, Olean* and *Caribsea*
Adolf Piening, Type IXC *U-155*: *Arabutan*
Reinhard Hardegen, Type IXB *U-123*: *Carolyn*
Heinrich Schuch, Type IXB *U-105*: *Narragansett*
Johannes Liebe, Type VIIC *U-332*: *Australia* and *Liberator*
Walter Flachsenberg, Type VIIC *U-71*: *Ranja* and *Dixie Arrow*

The *Arabutan*

The first ship to go down off the North Carolina coast in March was the 7,900-ton freighter *Arabutan*. At about nine o'clock on the night of the seventh, *U-155*, captained by Adolf Piening, fired a stern torpedo that, after a 102-second run, hit the ship, causing it to sink in about thirteen minutes. The ship had been spotted an hour earlier by the lookouts on the *U-155*, and the fact that it was from the neutral country of Brazil was discounted or wasn't noticed. Only one crew member died, and the rest of the fifty-four crew members escaped on four lifeboats. They were sighted by an aircraft about six hours later. The following day, the survivors were picked up by the coast guard cutter USS *Calypso* and taken to Little Creek, Virginia.

The *Caribsea*

The sinking of the *Caribsea* still has special significance for folks living on Ocracoke Island. Few are still living there who remember what happened about forty miles southwest of the island on the night of March 11 and on Ocracoke on the fourteenth.

Around midnight on the eleventh, Erwin Rostin and his *U-158* started patrolling the nearshore waters off Cape Lookout. He had just arrived after a fifty-eight-day stormy trip from France and was looking for the many ships he had been told would be passing by this spot heading to and from Cape Hatteras.

Nearing his location and traveling blacked out at a slow five miles an hour, the 2,600-ton freighter *Caribsea* creeped along in the direction of Diamond Shoals. Its captain, Nicholas Manolis, had been given orders by the navy to pass Cape Hatteras during daylight hours to avoid being attacked by a U-boat. The Cape passage was still more than six hours away, and this was the reason for the slow speed. Apparently, no thought was given to the fact that the U-boats were spread out all along the coast.

As it was after midnight, most of the twenty-eight-man crew were asleep below decks. This included third mate Jim Baum Gaskill. Gaskill, a native of Ocracoke, knew that he was near his home and could have stayed on the bridge of the freighter and watched for the light from the lighthouse on Silver Lake that was next to his father's hotel. He didn't.

Caribsea, sunk near Cape Lookout by *U-158*. *National Archives.*

Rostin's lookouts had spotted the 250-foot-long *Caribsea* but didn't know what to make of it. Rostin came to the bridge to take a look for himself. At first he thought the ship might be a coast guard cutter lying in wait or some type of U-boat trap. After thinking it over, he decided to go ahead with the attack.

It was about one thirty in the morning when a torpedo struck the *Caribsea*. The massive explosions that followed blew the ship to bits. Carrying highly combustible manganese ore, it was gone before any lifeboats could be launched or SOS signals could be made. The two crew members in the wheelhouse and six other men from below decks were able to get off the ship before it sank and cling to pieces of debris floating in the water. Jim Baum Gaskill was not among them.

The men in the sea were fortunate enough to come across a drifting life raft that had been blown overboard when the ship exploded. Records indicate that one man was unable to reach the raft and drowned. The seven others piled in and began to drift with the current. It was about two thirty in the morning, and land was forty miles away.

Rostin decided to hang around a while and circled the life raft for several hours. He never approached the men or tried to question them about which boat he had sunk and what they were carrying. As the dawn approached, he left, submerged, and headed south toward the Cape Fear area.

A freighter bound for Hampton Roads, the *Norlindo*, picked up the men on the raft and took them to a rendezvous with a coast guard dispatch boat. The dispatch boat took them to the Little Creek Coast Guard Station. All would live to tell their stories.

Back on Ocracoke Island several days later, the story goes that an oar with the name *Caribsea* on it and a wooden frame with Jim Baum Gaskill's third mate license inside washed ashore in Silver Lake near his father's hotel, the Pamlico Inn. Just how the oar and frame managed to travel over forty miles and get through the inlet into Silver Lake is still unexplained. A cross would later be fashioned from the oar and still can be found on the altar of the Ocracoke Methodist Church.

The *John D. Gill*

Rostin and his *U-158* spent the day on the bottom after the *Caribsea* sinking and proceeded south on the surface the following night. They were about fifteen miles southeast of Carolina Beach when the watch spotted a large ship moving in their general direction. Before long, they could see that it was a large tanker and appeared to be fully loaded.

The ship, the 530-foot *John D. Gill*, was loaded with 150,000 barrels of crude oil and was heading to Philadelphia. Its captain had been ordered to wait off Charleston for further orders due to the U-boat activity that had just taken place off the North Carolina coast. For some reason, the ship proceeded northeast anyway and rounded Cape Fear about ten o'clock at night on the twelfth. The sea was calm, and the ship was traveling just inside the Frying Pan Shoals Lightship Buoy. The forty-two-man crew and the seven navy gunners who were on board to man the two five-inch guns were still at their stations.

At about ten o'clock, Rostin fired a single torpedo from his position on the south side of the *Gill* and hit the ship on its starboard side in the number seven tank. Fuel oil immediately began to pour into the sea and surround the ship. As the *Gill* began to list, the order to abandon ship was given, although there was no immediate danger of it sinking. A crew member, not thinking about what he was doing, threw a life ring with a self-igniting carbide light over the side. When the light lit, the spark caused the oil in the water to burn furiously and soon engulf the whole ship. The starboard lifeboats were immediately consumed by the flames. This left the two port lifeboats and a smaller life raft available to save the captain, navy gunners and crew. One of these boats was lowered safely and was rowed by fifteen crew members away from the burning ship. The other lifeboat with fifteen more men jammed on the way down and dumped these folks into the burning sea. Some of these men would be cut to pieces as they were drawn into the blades of the still turning propeller. The remaining life raft was thrown overboard, and eight crew members and three navy gunners climbed in and eventually reached safety away from the burning oil.

The *Gill* remained afloat for another five hours. A series of tremendous explosions finally sent it to the bottom. Nineteen crew members and four navy gunners died with the ship.

The survivors in the lifeboat were picked up by the tanker *Robert H. Colley* and taken to Charleston, South Carolina. The men on the raft were picked up by a coast guard patrol boat and taken to Southport.

As for Rostin, he reversed course and headed for Cape Lookout, where he would find and sink the *Ario*.

The *Ario*

Early on the morning of March 15, the 6,952-ton tanker *Ario* was en route to Texas in ballast about eleven miles west of the Cape Lookout Buoy when it was struck by a torpedo from *U-158*, hitting on its starboard side. The number nine tank was ruptured, but since it was in water ballast, no fire or additional explosion occurred. A signal was sent by the radio operator that *Ario* had been attacked by a U-boat, and the thirty-six-man crew began to prepare to abandon ship.

Although the *Ario* was not armed and no defensive action was taken by the crew, Rostin began to shell the ship with his deck gun. One of the lifeboats that was being lowered into the sea was hit, killing eight of its occupants.

After firing numerous shells into the *Ario*, Rostin moved in and circled the ship for a while and then took off to the east. He was one of the few U-boat captains to shell unarmed sailors trying to escape their sinking vessel.

Soon after *U-158* departed, several of the crew reboarded the *Ario* and checked to see if a salvage attempt should be made. They concluded that the

Ario, sunk near Cape Lookout by *U-158*. *National Archives.*

Ario would soon sink and went back to their lifeboat. About eight hours later, the survivors were picked up by a destroyer and taken to Charleston, South Carolina. It took the *Ario* more than fifteen hours to sink, but it finally went down about ten miles east of Cape Lookout.

The *British Resource*

Kapitanleutnant Johann Mohr and his Type IXB *U-124* left France on February 21 and neared the North Carolina coastline on March 14. He had taken the direct route to Hatteras, passing close to Bermuda on the way. Now he was only two hundred miles from the American shoreline and didn't want to give his position away and possibly spoil his chances where he knew that the ships were. This was his plan until late on the evening of the fourteenth, when his lookouts spotted what appeared to be a large tanker dead ahead. It was the 7,200-ton tanker *British Resource*, carrying over

10,000 tons of benzene and white spirit. After seeing the ship himself, Moyer decided to torpedo it and sent three torpedoes west, resulting in a terrific explosion that rose over five hundred feet in the air, setting the entire ship on fire and causing the *Resource* to sink the following day. Of the fifty-one crewmen on board, only five survived. They were picked up two days later by the HMS *Clarkia* and taken to Hamilton, Bermuda.

Mohr circled the burning ship and dying men until he could identify his victim as the *Resource* and then took off for the North Carolina coast. By the following night, he was just eighty miles east of Diamond Shoals and Cape Hatteras. Still heading west, his lookouts again spotted a ship. This one was not as large as the *Resource* but presented an easy target.

THE *CEIBA*

The *Ceiba* was a 1,700-ton freighter owned by the Standard Fruit Company of New Orleans. On the night of the sixteenth, the ship was steaming along at about thirteen miles an hour, heading for New York with a full load of bananas. Moyer fired a single torpedo from one of his bow tubes that hit with such force that it almost turned the ship over.

The crew had time to launch two lifeboats and a raft before the ship went down. Many of the people on board, mostly Hondurans, drowned as Mohr circled trying to find out which ship he had sunk. In a sea of floating bananas and screaming survivors, he questioned several men in one of the lifeboats about the ship's tonnage and cargo. When he found out that the cargo was totally bananas and that *Ceiba* was fewer than two thousand tons, he became furious and left without trying to help anyone in the sea. He soon dove and again headed for the Carolina coastline.

Of the fifty people on board, only six would survive that terrible night. The three boats became separated, and two of them and their occupants were never seen again. The six men on the raft were picked up by the USS *Hambleton* two days later.

THE *AUSTRALIA*

The *Australia* was the second-largest ship sunk off the coast of North Carolina during World War II. The tanker was 510 feet long and weighed 11,600 tons. Owned by Texaco, the ship had been loaded with 110,000 barrels of oil at Port Arthur, Texas, and was heading for New Haven, Connecticut, when the attack occurred.

Ordered to round Cape Hatteras during daylight hours, the *Australia* was about thirty miles east of the Cape on the afternoon of the sixteenth when a torpedo fired by *U-332* struck its starboard side in the engine room. Traveling during daylight hours had done no good. Four crewmen of the forty-man complement were killed instantly when the torpedo exploded.

Captain Ader, who was on the bridge of the *Australia*, and thirty-five of the remaining crew were able to escape in three lifeboats. Although the oil didn't ignite, the ship went down several hours later in eighty feet of water. Adler and the other survivors were rescued less than two hours later by the *William J. Salman* and taken to Southport, North Carolina.

Johannes Liebe left France on February 17 and reached the Hatteras area ahead of Mohr on March 15. His boat, the Type VIIC *U-332*, was smaller and carried less fuel than Mohr's Type IXs. When he finally arrived in American waters, he only had six days to launch his attacks before he had to begin his return trip. He would make good use of his time and sink four ships before returning to France.

Captain Johann Mohr of *U-124*. *Bundesarchiv, Koblenz*.

Liebe was running at periscope depth when he saw the *Australia*. The ship was zigzagging and moving alone at about twelve miles an hour. After sending one torpedo into its engine room, he decided to hang around until it sank. This almost proved to be a fatal mistake for Liebe, his boat and his crew.

The *Dione*, a large coast guard cutter that had been patrolling the Hatteras area, received a call requesting help for the *Australia* that was currently being attacked by a U-boat only twenty miles away. It took the *Dione* a little more than an hour to spot the sinking ship. Within two hours, the sonar operator had picked up an echo from the *U-332*, and the *Dione* made ready for a depth charge attack. Liebe was submerged in only eighty feet of water and could make no more than six miles an hour with his electric motors. It looked like a victory for the *Dione* was almost a certainty.

When the sonar operator finally located the spot in the ocean that he thought was just above the submerged U-boat, Captain Alger, the captain of

Australia, sunk by *U-332* east of Cape Hatteras. The *Australia* was the second-largest vessel sunk off the coast of North Carolina during World War II. *National Archives.*

the *Dione*, gave the order to drop depth charges. Nothing came up from the sea floor but mud. Somehow, Liebe had done the impossible and escaped.

Mohr and his *U-124* had finally reached Hatteras. It was late in the afternoon of the seventeenth when he caught sight of the Diamond Shoals Buoy marking the edge of the shipping lanes. In less than an hour, his lookouts spotted several ships coming down from the north. From the bridge, he counted what appeared to be three merchantmen and two escorts appearing to be the lead ships of a convoy. He had been told that the United States Navy had not started convoying yet, and he was right. The ships had randomly joined together as they neared Cape Hatteras. The coast guard cutter *Dione* and the destroyer *Dickerson* also just happened to be in the area. Mohr submerged and waited for the tankers to pass by.

First to be hit was the 6,800-ton *Acme*. The ship, with a crew of thirty-one, was heading from New York to Corpus Christi, Texas, in ballast. The torpedo exploded beneath the engine room and rocked the ship from side to side, blasting a hole forty feet wide in the hull. The explosion killed eleven men who were in the engine room and crew's quarters. The twenty survivors immediately abandoned ship and were picked up by the *Dione* within thirty minutes. The ship settled on the shallow bottom and was later towed to Newport News, Virginia, where it was repaired and returned to service.

Mohr immediately crash-dived to the eighty-foot sandy bottom and waited. Two navy aircraft were circling, and the *Dickerson* began to search the area with sonar. Again it looked like a U-boat would finally be sunk. It didn't happen. Mohr, in spite of a depth charge attack nearby by the *Dickerson* and the several navy aircraft flying overhead, immediately ordered the boat back to periscope depth and prepared for another attack.

Kassandra Louloudis

The five-thousand-ton Greek freighter *Kassandra*, following close behind the *Acme*, soon passed the burning hull. The captain, Themistokles Mitlas, ordered his ship to begin zigzagging and come to full speed. Pulling away from the *Acme* and heading west, someone on the bridge thought he saw a fin cutting the water ahead. It was the attack periscope of the *U-124*.

Mohr fired two torpedoes. One missed, but the second one struck the port side of the freighter. The ship's engine continued to run, but the steering gear was ruined. It was time to abandon ship. All thirty-five of the crew survived

Acme, sunk by *U-124* near Diamond Shoals light. *National Archives.*

and were picked up by the *Dione*. The cutter now had more survivors than crew members aboard. They would all be taken to Norfolk, Virginia. The ship sank to the shallow bottom about 2:00 a.m. and came to rest upright with both its masts and funnel sticking out of the water.

Mohr still had the *Dickerson* and the *Dione* to contend with but was again able to escape their frantic search for him. He decided to leave the immediate area and head southwest. Maybe he could spot a ship or two coming up the coast south of Diamond Shoals.

E.M. CLARK

A few hours after the *Kassandra* went down, the *Clark* was nearing Diamond Shoals. It was unaware of what had just happened only a few miles ahead. Steaming from Baton Rouge, Louisiana, with 119,000 barrels of heating oil, the 9,600-ton tanker was en route to New York. With a crew of forty-

177. Kapitänleutnant Johann Mohr.
Als Sohn eines Senators und Stadtbaurats in Hannover 1916 geboren. 1934 Eintritt in die Kriegsmarine. 1940 Erster Wachoffizier auf einem U-Boot. Zeichnete sich auch in gefahrvoller Lage des Bootes durch umsichtiges und unerschrockenes Verhalten aus. Als Kommandant eines U-Bootes versenkte er den britischen Kreuzer „Dunedin" sowie 16 bewaffnete feindliche Handelsschiffe mit 103 405 BRT. In der Folgezeit vernichtete er erneut 17 bewaffnete feindliche Handelsschiffe mit 84 600 BRT. Bewies bereits auf seiner ersten Feindfahrt im Angriff gegen zwei Geleitzüge sein hervorragendes Können. Blitzschnelle Entschlußkraft, gestützt auf große technische Erfahrung, sichern ihm überlegene Erfolge. Ritterkreuz am 27. 3. 1942; Eichenlaub am 13. 1. 1943.

A newspaper article about Captain Mohr. *Wolfgang Klue.*

one men, all seemed well as the ship sailed along at a slow ten miles an hour. A winter thunderstorm had been producing lightning for several hours that was bright enough to light up the sky and the ship.

Mohr fired his first torpedo about 4:00 a.m. He was at least ten miles away from where the *Kassandra* sank and was not worried about the *Dickerson* or *Dione* finding him. The torpedo struck the port side of the ship. Captain Hubert Hassel heard the muffled explosion. He was in bed but quickly got up and made his way to the bridge. After getting a damage report, he went to the radio room to get a message out about the torpedo attack. Finding out that the main antenna had been damaged by the first torpedo, he ordered the radio operator to attempt an emergency repair. While this was being done, a second explosion, much louder than the first, rocked the ship. The holds containing the oil had been ruptured, and oil was pouring out into the sea. This would be the fatal blow that would send the *Clark* to the bottom. All but one of the forty-one-man crew would survive. They would be picked up on the morning of the eighteenth by the *Dickerson*, which had finally arrived, and carried to Ocracoke.

Engrossed in rescuing survivors of the *Acme, Kassandra* and *Clark*, neither the *Dickerson* nor the *Dione* had been able to carry out any kind of coordinated attack on the *U-124*. Mohr did receive a scare when a navy seaplane dropped two depth charges close enough to rock his boat as it lay on the bottom. He decided he had had enough for the time being and headed out to deeper water for a rest. He would be back by nightfall.

Mohr returned to his shallow hunting grounds along the twenty-meter line soon after the sun set on the eighteenth. Traveling on the surface, he decided to wait and watch between the Cape Hatteras Lighthouse and Cape Lookout. He would encounter two tankers and sink them both in less than an hour. They were the *Papoose* and the *E.H. Hutton*.

The *Papoose*

The 5,900-ton tanker *Papoose* was heading for Corpus Christi, Texas, in water ballast to pick up a load of fuel oil. On the night of the eighteenth, the ship had rounded Cape Hatteras and was nearing Cape Lookout when it was spotted by the *U-124*'s watches. Captain Zalnic and the thirty-three-man crew were glad to be past the Diamond Shoals and weren't expecting the torpedo that struck the port side at 9:30 p.m. They were traveling about twelve miles an hour and zigzagging in sixty feet of water when the sudden explosion ripped out interior bulkheads, penetrated a fuel tank and let oil and water flow into the engine room. Within four minutes, this mixture rose above the cylinder heads, and the damaged engine stopped.

The radio operator was able to get a message out indicating that the ship had been torpedoed about fifteen miles southwest of Cape Lookout and was sinking. The first lifeboat was launched within five minutes after the attack. The survivors immediately observed *U-124* approaching their ship and

Papoose, sunk off Cape Lookout by *U-124*. *National Archives.*

circling around it to observe the damage. Pulling away, Mohr fired a second torpedo that ripped a second huge hole in the ship, sending debris flying. The second lifeboat was finally launched shortly after the second torpedo hit with the rest of the crew. Two of the thirty-four-man crew died on the ship, and the rest were rescued by the destroyer *Stringham* at seven thirty the next morning.

Mohr was reported to have now said, "We're on the land side of her [*Papoose*] and we'd have more water under us in a bathtub than we've got here." He ordered the *U-124* wheeled around and headed for deeper water. Its crew would all breathe easier with a safe depth under its hull.

As the boat turned southwestward heading for the open sea, the lookouts spotted another tanker. This one appeared to be fully loaded. It was the *E.H. Hutton*.

E.H. HUTTON

The seven-thousand-ton tanker *Hutton* was proceeding northeast with a crew of thirty-six and sixty-five thousand barrels of heating oil, heading for Marcus Hook, Pennsylvania. Captain Carl Flaathen had been keeping his ship inshore near the fifteen-fathom line and in sight of the nearshore buoys. He, like most of the other captains, thought that U-boats were afraid or unable to operate in water this shallow. He was apparently unaware that most of the attacks were carried out from the surface at night and the shallow water only became dangerous if the U-boat were found by surface craft. As an extra precaution, he had ordered all the portholes blacked out and posted extra watches.

Mohr approached the *Hutton* on the surface, set up for a bow tube shot and fired his first torpedo. It was about ten o'clock when the first torpedo, fired from about eight hundred meters away, hit. A lookout had seen it coming but too late to do anything about it. The explosion, on the starboard side of the ship, buckled the bow, flooded the forward tanks and carried away both anchors. A second torpedo was fired a minute or so after the first one and either was a dud or missed.

The ship, now stopped in the water, did not immediately sink. The radioman was able to get off a distress signal that was quickly acknowledged. Mohr was listening on the six-hundred-meter band and knew that a destroyer would be there soon. He fired his third torpedo immediately, knowing that the time he could safely expose his boat on the surface was running out. The explosion that followed when the torpedo hit set the oil on fire, destroyed the pilot house and set most of the ship on fire.

The thirty-six-man crew was still trying to abandon ship. Thirteen of these men were lost, either burning to death on the ship or in the sea of flaming oil. The rest were able to climb into two lifeboats and two rafts before the ship went down less than an hour after the initial blast.

The following morning, all of the survivors were able to pile in one lifeboat and begin rowing toward shore. They were picked up by the British freighter MV *Port Halifax*.

Mohr had sunk two ships in less than an hour and decided to retire for the rest of the night. Heading out into deep water, he put the *U-124* on the bottom and let his men get some needed sleep.

Meanwhile, the destroyer *Dickerson* was on the way. Still more than forty miles away and plowing west at thirty miles an hour, it would be too late to do anything about Mohr but watch the burning oil that still lit up the sea where the *Hutton* and the *Papoose* went down.

The *Liberator*

The captain of the 7,700-ton freighter *Liberator* carrying a load of sulfur knew that there was going to be trouble ahead. Steaming east with a thirty-five-man crew and heading for New York, Captain Albin Johnson already knew about the recent sinkings along his route. He had hastily alerted the four-man navy gun crew to be ready for quick action. The four-inch gun on the ship's fantail and the navy armed guard that manned it were more than capable of sinking a U-boat.

As the ship approached the Cape Lookout area, the lookouts on the *Liberator* could see the burning remains of the *Hutton* several miles ahead. Flames from the burning oil reached several hundred feet into the night sky. The captain considered turning back at this point but continued ahead, zigzagging at twelve miles an hour

The *Dickerson*, still in route and heading west, was blacked out and making almost thirty miles an hour. Its captain and crew could also see the burning oil five miles ahead. *Dickerson* and *Liberator* were on a collision course.

Around three o'clock in the morning, one of the lookouts on the *Liberator* spotted what he thought was a U-boat running at high speed on the surface.

As the distance between the two vessels closed, the gun crew on the *Liberator* fired a shell in the direction of the approaching ship. The ship was not a U-boat but the *Dickerson*.

The shell struck the *Dickerson*'s bridge, passed through the chart room and exploded in the radio room. Three men were killed instantly and seven more injured. One of the critically hurt was the *Dickerson*'s captain, Lieutenant Commander J.K. Reybold. The ship's executive officer, Lieutenant F.E. Wilson, immediately took charge. He turned the *Dickerson* around and headed for Norfolk, Virginia. He didn't realize that his gyro compass had been damaged by the explosion for over fifteen minutes and he was actually heading south. Finally utilizing his magnetic compass, he got the boat going in the right direction.

It was after three o'clock the following afternoon when the *Dickerson* approached Cape Henry with the wounded men. Unfortunately, Reybold died a short time later.

Just after ten o'clock in the morning of the nineteenth, the *Liberator* approached Diamond Shoals. The light buoy could be seen several miles ahead. The captain decided to pass on the land side of the buoy where the water was shallower. He would be happy with forty feet under his hull thinking that no U-boat would dare operate on the surface here or be able to launch a submerged attack in such shallow water. He was still making over ten miles an hour but discontinued zigzagging.

Just ahead waited Johannes Liebe and his *U-332*. He was not only on the surface but also on the shallower land side of the passing *Liberator*. He only had to fire one torpedo to do the job. It struck the ship in the engine room about twenty feet below the waterline. The explosion destroyed the engine and blew up the decking above it. One lifeboat was destroyed and five men were killed instantly. The others manned the two remaining lifeboats and abandoned the ship within ten minutes after the torpedo struck. The ship sank to the bottom in less than twenty. The survivors were picked up by the USS *Umpaqua* in less than an hour and taken to Morehead City.

The navy armed guard gun crew still thought that they had damaged and possibly sunk a U-boat. No official report indicating that they had actually shelled the *Dickerson* was ever made.

THE *NAECO*

On the morning of March 23, Johann Mohr had two torpedoes left. He had already sunk seven ships during the nine days he terrorized the North Carolina coast and intended to get at least one more.

Patrolling between Cape Fear and Cape Lookout about one o'clock in the morning, his lookouts spotted a ship proceeding east at twelve miles an hour. The ship was alone, and Mohr saw that it was a tanker, the five-thousand-ton *Naeco*. With a crew of thirty-eight and a cargo of kerosene and heating oil, the ship was traveling from Houston, Texas, to Seawarren, New Jersey.

Mohr was able to overtake the ship in an hour and set up for a bow shot. When the *Naeco* crossed in front of him and was about nine hundred meters away, he ordered one torpedo fired from his bow tubes. He had spent most of the previous day checking the two torpedoes and was sure that they were ready for firing.

The torpedo hit the *Naeco* squarely amidships, but no explosion occurred. It was, in fact, a dud. Captain Emil Engelbrecht, apparently unaware of the U-boat's presence, continued along just south of the Cape Lookout Shoals. Mohr again had to maneuver ahead of the *Naeco* and wait for another opportunity to shoot. It came about 3:00 a.m.

The last torpedo slammed into the starboard side of the *Naeco*. The 100,000 barrels of oil and kerosene the ship was carrying ignited and exploded with a fury that sent flames shooting three hundred feet in the air. The bridge and most of its superstructure were destroyed immediately. The captain and all the duty officers there were gone, either blown to bits or incinerated by the fire.

Complete confusion consumed those left alive on the tanker. Some men were immediately burned to death and others killed trying to escape in lifeboats. The ship broke in two and separated while still afloat. Men were jumping into the sea and being burned to death by the flaming oil that surrounded the ship. The one lifeboat that survived the fall to the ocean was all that was able to provide refuge for the screaming men.

Ten men got away from the ship in this lifeboat and were picked up about four hours later by the *Dione*. Two others were also found alive in the sea. The minesweeper *Osprey* picked up four bodies and one survivor from a raft. The boatswain, who had returned and climbed back on the *Naeco*, was miraculously rescued by the tug *Umpaqua*. They were all carried to Morehead City. In the end, there were twenty-four dead and fourteen survivors.

Naeco, sunk south of Cape Lookout by *U-124*. *National Archives.*

The Germans on the bridge of *U-124* watched silently from a distance as the *Naeco* burned. The intense heat created by the explosions and fires made it impossible to get very close. The men on the sub knew that there was no catastrophe at sea that could compare to a burning tanker and no more horrible and inescapable death for a merchant seaman. They tried to concentrate on the fact that fuel destroyed by them could not be used against German forces in the future. All they could really think of was that sailors like themselves were burning and dying in the flames.

Before dawn, Mohr ordered his *U-124* down and headed east toward France. That night, he radioed Donitz that his torpedoes were gone and he had had great success during his patrol. He described the heavy traffic, mostly tankers, that passed Cape Hatteras during the morning and evening and said that during the night, ships would go from Hatteras to Cape Fear. There was no nighttime traffic between Cape Fear and Charleston. Ships steered from one buoy to the next without entering the bays, and light and radio beacons were in operation as though it were peacetime. Destroyers and coast guard cutters patrolled around Hatteras and on the shipping lanes, and planes appeared in the evenings. There were no mines.

He also sent Donitz this message: "Hunters thanks for a free hunt. In the stormy new moon light—was by Lookout the tanker fight. The poor Roosevelt lost fifty thousand tons."

Several hours later, he received Donitz's reply: "Well done," with the notification that he would be awarded the Knight's Cross upon his arrival home. The award signified that he had sunk at least 100,000 tons of shipping.

The *Dixie Arrow*

Mohr had sailed for France on the twenty-fourth. One of the U-boats sent to replace him had already arrived on the twentieth.

Walter Flachsenberg, in his Type VIIC *U-71*, wasted no time getting started. On the twentieth, he sank the 6,400-ton tanker *Ranja* and the 5,700-ton freighter *Oakmar* three hundred miles northeast of Cape Hatteras. He continued moving toward Diamond Shoals and arrived there on the twenty-second. By the morning of the twenty-third, he was in position near the spot of so many sinkings in the past sixty days: the Diamond Shoals Light Buoy.

He was just about ready to leave for deeper water and spend some time on the bottom when one of his lookouts spotted a ship in the distance. It was coming up from the southwest and looked like it might be a tanker. It was.

The ship was the eight-thousand-ton *Dixie Arrow*, heading for Paulsboro, New Jersey, and fully loaded with ninety-six thousand barrels of crude oil. Its captain, Anders Johanson, had taken the precaution of zigzagging. Initially, he had intended to pass the Cape blacked out and at night. He would now pass during daylight hours instead. The thirty-three-man crew was nervous about the whole situation but continued on in the sunlight.

Flachsenberg had submerged and planned to attack as the *Arrow* passed between him and the shore. He would use his bow torpedo tubes and fire three of the four torpedoes. He wanted to be sure that the *Dixie Arrow* went down.

It was about nine o'clock in the morning when the first torpedo was seen approaching the tanker by one of the lookouts. The sky was clear and the sea calm, making the trail of bubbles easy to spot. The *Arrow*'s helmsman called for the ship to make a radical turn away from the approaching torpedo, but it was too late.

Dixie Arrow burning. It was sunk by *U-71* near the Diamond Shoals Light Buoy. *National Archives.*

The first torpedo hit amidships on the starboard side and ignited the oil. A tremendous fireball shot toward the sky, engulfing everything around it. The deckhouse was destroyed and all the deck officers killed. Within seconds, another torpedo hit, stopping the engines, killing several more of the crew and sending the others running for the bow, which was not yet engulfed by the flames.

Oscar Chappel, who was the helmsman, realized that the fire pushed forward by the wind would soon reach these men and burn them alive. He decided that the only solution would be to turn the boat into the wind, which immediately brought the flames back toward him. He burned to death minutes later in this selfless act.

One more torpedo finished the job. The captain, most of the officers and many of the crew members had been killed. The radio operator and the radio had been incinerated, and no distress signal was transmitted. The barrels of oil had been destroyed, and all that remained of the ship was a burning mass of steel. Two of the four lifeboats had been burned up in the fire, and one swamped when it broke loose and hit the water. Only one was left to save the remaining survivors.

Eight men made it into this boat, and the rest were left to cling to hatch covers or other debris. One raft was launched but drifted toward the fire, and all but one man abandoned it. The remaining crew member apparently couldn't swim and stayed with the raft as it drifted into the fire. He and the raft were consumed quickly in the blazing sea.

The one lifeboat and the drifting men in the sea were slowly being taken away from the burning *Dixie Arrow* by the current. In about an hour, they spotted a ship approaching from the south. It was the destroyer USS *Tarbell*. The *Tarbell* had been operating in the general area and had seen the fireball and smoke from the burning ship rising high in the sky.

Watching the *Arrow* burn through his periscope, Flachsenberg also saw the *Tarbell* approaching. He knew that the destroyer would be above him in minutes and dropping depth charges that could mean his end. He ordered the leading engineer to take the *U-71* down and to head for deeper water with the best speed he could make.

The *Tarbell*'s sonar located the U-boat quickly, and a barrage of depth charges was dropped. *U-71* was badly shaken but somehow managed to escape.

The *Tarbell*'s captain, Lieutenant Commander S.D. Willigham, felt compelled to break off the attack and rescue the men he now saw all around him in the sea. He would pick up twenty-two live crewmen and take them to Morehead City.

The *Dixie Arrow* continued to drift southwest long after the men were gone. It finally came to rest on the bottom in ninety feet of water about twelve miles southeast of Hatteras Inlet.

The *City of New York*

Kapitan Georg Lassen left France on February 24 with his Type IXC *U-160* bound for Cape Hatteras. On the way over, he came across the Panamanian freighter *Equipoise* about fifty miles southeast of Cape Henry on the night of the twenty-seventh. The ship had a crew of fifty-three and was heading for Baltimore with a load of manganese ore. It was an old freighter built in 1903 and could only make about eight miles an hour. *Equipoise* was no match for Lassen. He fired one torpedo into the starboard side, and it sank within two minutes. Only thirteen men survived. It would be Lassen's first victory in American waters.

His first victim after his arrival east of the Diamond Shoals was the 8,300-ton cargo-passenger ship *City of New York* with 123 people on board; 47 of these were passengers. There were also 9 men of the navy's armed guard on board.

On the afternoon of the twenty-ninth, the ship was plowing along with a load of chrome ore about forty miles east of Hatteras, heading for New York. The sea was extremely rough and limited speed to less than fifteen miles an hour. Lassen was waiting submerged just ahead. As he sat in the conning tower looking through his periscope, he saw the ship coming up from the west. When the ship passed in front of him, he fired his first torpedo and scored a hit just below the bridge on the port side. Not only did the explosion rip a large hole below the waterline, but it also destroyed all shipboard communication. The captain, George Sullivan, immediately had the engines shut down. The ship was now drifting in the wind.

Equipoise, sunk off Currituck Lighthouse by *U-160*. Mariners Museum, Newport News, Virginia.

One of the six lifeboats on board had also been destroyed. The others were made ready for lowering, and the passengers began scrambling into them.

The navy armed guards who had been standing by their four-inch gun spotted Lassen's periscope and began firing shells in an attempt to disable it. They were not successful, and the U-boat circled around the ship and launched another torpedo that penetrated the starboard side. The explosion caused one of the remaining five lifeboats that was being lowered into the sea to fall rapidly and hit the water hard, dumping the inhabitants into the sea. The remaining four boats were lowered safely before the *City of New York* sank stern first twenty minutes later.

Lassen watched the ship go down from several hundred feet away. He must have also seen the four surviving lifeboats and three life rafts bouncing around in the twelve-foot seas. He soon withdrew to calmer, deeper water.

The next day, a PBY Catalina aircraft searched the area of the sinking but found nothing. Thirty-six hours after the sinking, three lifeboats and seventy survivors were picked up by the destroyer USS *Roper*. Twenty-nine more were picked up by the USS *Acushnet*. All were taken to the Naval Base in Norfolk, Virginia.

On April 11, a U.S. Army bomber spotted the fourth lifeboat. Eleven survivors were picked up by a coast guard vessel and brought in to Lewes, Delaware.

In the end, one armed guard, sixteen crewmen and seven passengers perished.

With this sinking, the bloody month of March ended.

CHAPTER 8

APRIL

More U-Boats Arrive and More Ships Go Down

Karl Donitz sent twenty-six U-boats to the Americas in March. They would start arriving along the East Coast early in April. Many of the captains running these boats were very experienced and had sunk over 100,000 tons of shipping. There were six Type IXs and twenty Type VIIs. Ten of these captains would sink eighteen ships off North Carolina by May 1.

The Germans had also come up with the idea of sending large U-tankers capable of refueling the U-boats on station. Two of these would operate several hundred miles off the coast in April. They were the *U-459* and the *U-A*.

U-459 was the first so-called milch cow stationed off the North Carolina coast and was used to resupply U-boats operating in the area. *National Archives.*

On the American side, ASW forces were increasing all the time, and Admiral Andrews had no fewer than five blimps, over one hundred aircraft and ninety auxiliary-type ships to patrol the Eastern Sea Frontier. Twenty destroyers were also made available by Admiral King for use on a part-time basis.

Two destroyers, the *Emmons* and the *Hambleton*, were released by Admiral Andrews to patrol the North Carolina coastline from Wimble Shoals to Cape Lookout. The Coast Guard cutter *Dione* would remain on patrol with them.

Reinhard Hardegen and *U-123* Return to the North Carolina Coast

The first of the six Type IX boats to return to the North Carolina coast was Reinhard Hardegen's. He left France on March 2 and neared the coast a little over three weeks later. Taking the direct route instead of the great circle, he passed Bermuda and was about two hundred miles east of Hatteras when he met with a surprise that almost ended his life and those of his crew.

On the afternoon of March 26, *U-123* came up on what appeared to be an old freighter making about eight miles an hour. He decided to sink it and fired one torpedo into the ship's side. The hit was solid, but the ship didn't appear to be sinking, although the lifeboats were lowered and the crew seemed to be leaving the ship. He decided to move in and finish the ship off with his deck gun.

As the *U-123* approached, part of the ship's superstructure appeared to fall away, revealing a large four-inch gun pointed right at the sub. The gun immediately started firing, depth charges were flung by K guns and several machine guns opened up on the surprised U-boat crew.

Hardegen, knowing that he could be sunk, ordered the *U-123* to submerge, which it did without serious damage. After regaining his composure, he lined up for a second torpedo attack, which was successful. The ship sank with the entire navy crew. None was ever seen again.

The freighter was not just a freighter. The ship, formerly the *Carolyn*, had been turned into the *Atik*, a new defensive weapon devised in secret by the navy to fight the U-boats. It was called a "Q" ship and was highly classified. At this time, only two had been built.

When an unsuspecting captain, this time Hardegen, brought his boat in close to finish the Q ship off, he would be met by a hail of fire, including depth charges that would, in fact, sink the U-boat. Unfortunately, it didn't work so well this time.

After almost losing his *U-123*, Hardegen was happy to finally be approaching Hatteras. On the night of March 30, he watched as the Hatteras Lighthouse welcomed him back. It was, however, not the same welcome he had had before.

During the next two days, he attacked three ships but failed to sink a single one. Increased air and sea patrols by the navy and coast guard drove him down constantly. His happy hunting ground had changed since January. He decided to move farther south away from North Carolina and shallow water.

Rio Blanco

The 4,000-ton freighter *Rio Blanco* left St. Thomas, Virgin Islands, on March 16 with 6,400 tons of iron ore. On April 1 around noon, it had rounded the shoals at Cape Hatteras and was proceeding north at eight knots through heavy seas. The fifty-two man crew was weary of the trip and ready to reach their destination of Hampton Roads, less than two hundred miles away.

Oberleutnant zur See Georg Lassen, captain of the *U-160*, had other plans for the *Rio Blanco*. He had remained in the area since sinking the *City of New York* on March 29 and was in good position to sink the *Rio Blanco*.

He fired one torpedo into the port side of the freighter that blew up the pilot house and radio room. The heavy load of iron ore helped take the ship to the bottom almost immediately, taking twenty-eight of the crew with it. No SOS was sent.

Two lifeboats and one raft somehow managed to get away from the ship before it sank. The captain of the *Blanco*, Aiden Blackett, was one of the survivors. The seas were extremely rough, and the shore was a distant sixty miles away. The twenty-four men in the lifeboats would drift for two weeks. Three more would die before they were all rescued by the British trawlers *Herdfordshire* and *Niagara*. Twelve men were landed in Norfolk, Virginia, and nine taken to Halifax, Nova Scotia.

Lassen would continue to work the Hatteras area until April 9, when he sank the *Malchase*.

Byron D. Benson

On the night of April 4, a newcomer to the area, Captain Erich Topp, brought his Type VIIC *U-552* to the surface just south of Currituck light and waited. He was only seven miles offshore and could see the lights of Nags Head and Manteo in the distance. It was early evening, and he had all night to hunt.

It wasn't long before his conning tower watch officer called, "Captain to the con." He had spotted what appeared to him to be a convoy of ships heading north and less than three miles away.

What he saw steaming toward him was the eight-thousand-ton tanker *Byron Benson* accompanied by two armed escorts: the USS *Hamilton* and the HMS *Norwich City*. Another tanker, the *Gulf of Mexico*, had also pulled up from behind and joined the group. The *Benson* would be the prize Topp would attack. The ship was an easy target: 465 feet long, carrying 100,000 barrels of crude oil and only making eight knots.

Topp got his boat in position outside the *Benson* and fired one torpedo into its starboard side. The explosion that resulted was extremely loud, and the flames that rose three hundred feet in the air could easily be seen from Duck all the way to Nags Head.

U-552. Bundesarchiv, Koblenz.

U-552 and Captain Erich Topp. *Bundesarchiv, Koblenz.*

Jim Anderson, who lived on the oceanfront in Kitty Hawk, reported that it shook his house so violently that he ran outside to see what had happened. Looking back toward the northeast, he saw a giant fireball rising in the sky.

Jim Wilkins, who was down from Elizabeth City for the weekend and staying in his cottage in Kitty Hawk, reported that a group of fishermen decided to use their large surfboat to row out to the fire and see if they could help the survivors. Upon reaching a point that was several miles from the beach, they heard what sounded like a diesel engine and saw a searchlight playing in their direction. Thinking that this might be the U-boat that had caused the fire, they turned around and rowed back to shore.

Back on the *Benson*, near panic had taken over. The men in the engine room left their stations before shutting down the engines. Crewmen trying to escape the flames found the starboard lifeboats gone and burning oil gushing out into the sea. Rushing across the ship to the port side, men were crowding into the two lifeboats that were still intact. The captain and nine men in one lifeboat made it into the sea, but because the *Benson* was still making headway, their boat drifted into the mass of burning oil around the stern. They were all burned to death.

Twenty-six men climbed into the other lifeboat, and they, too, made it down and into the sea. Realizing that their boat was in the path of the

Byron D. Benson just after being hit by a torpedo from the *U-552*. *National Archives.*

Byron D. Benson in flames, sunk off Duck by *U-552*. *National Archives.*

Byron D. Benson completely engulfed in smoke and flame. *National Archives.*

burning oil, they used all the strength they had to pull away from the ship and escape the fate of the other boat.

Four officers and twenty-one crewmen in one boat were picked up within two hours by the *Hamilton*. One crewman on a raft was picked up by the *Norwich City*, and the last survivor was picked up by the coast guard cutter *Dione*. All the survivors were taken to Norfolk.

Topp, who would sink more ships off North Carolina in April than any other U-boat captain, moved slowly away from the area, surfaced and headed south toward Cape Hatteras.

The *Benson* burned and drifted southeast for three days before finally sinking in 110 feet of water east of Duck.

As before, even with three armed vessels in the immediate area of a sinking, no U-boat was found.

BRITISH SPLENDOUR

Before the *Byron D. Benson* came to rest on the bottom off Duck, Topp and his *U-552* were waiting on the surface east of Diamond Shoals looking for another victim. It was the evening of April 6.

About eleven o'clock, Topp was called to the conning tower by his watch officer. Looking southwest, he could see the shape of a large ship and a smaller one moving toward him. It was the *British Splendour* and the HMS *Zeno*.

The seven-thousand-ton tanker *British Splendour* was heading for England with ten thousand gallons of gasoline it had picked up from Houston, Texas. It had to pass Cape Hatteras and head up the coast to Halifax, where a convoy was being formed to cross the Atlantic. Leased to the British Ministry of Shipping to help England's war effort, the ship was being accompanied by the armed British trawler HMS *Zeno* for protection against U-boats. Both ships were running blacked out and making about ten knots as they approached Cape Hatteras. The seas were calm and the sky clear.

It had been decided that the *Splendour* would pass just east of the shoals and the *Zeno* would guard its starboard side and stay just ahead and at a distance of one mile. The fifty-three-man crew was on high alert with a seven-man lookout watching the water and a two-man crew manning the four-inch gun on the stern.

Topp, seeing what the two ships were up to, maneuvered the *U-552* to a spot just east of the shoals but inside the spot where the *Splendour* would pass. As the ships went by him, he fired a single torpedo from his forward tubes that struck the port side of the *Splendour* just behind the engine room. The explosion destroyed the engines, blew the section of the ship just aft of the engines to pieces and killed twelve crewmen who were in the engine room.

The ship came to a complete stop, and the crew was ordered to abandon ship. The captain and the remaining forty crew members made it off the ship without incident and were immediately picked up by the *Zeno* and taken to Norfolk. The ship sank in less than two hours and came to rest in 110 feet of water.

Topp watched as the *British Splendour* burned and sank and the *Zeno* pulled away with the survivors. He decided to hang around for the rest of the night.

The SS *Lancing*

Topp stayed in the vicinity of the attack on the *British Splendour* until just before sunrise on April 7. He then took off for deeper water and a day of rest on the bottom.

Not long after running south and away from the coast, he was again called to the conning tower. His lookouts had spotted another ship off *U-552*'s stern. It was the *Lancing.* Topp ordered the U-boat turned around and headed back toward the coast. He ran at a full twenty miles an hour until he was several miles east of the *Lansing* and waited patiently on the surface just seaward of where he expected the ship to pass.

The 470-foot-long *Lancing* was originally a whale factory ship that during peacetime carried whale oil. It now had been converted to carry fuel oil and was heading for New York with nine thousand tons of this commodity. The ship had a crew of fifty men and was armed with one four-inch gun and six heavy machine guns. Moving along at ten miles an hour, the *Lancing*'s captain planned to pass around Cape Hatteras during daylight but never made it that far.

Just before sunrise, Topp fired one torpedo that hit the *Lancing* just below the waterline, blowing a large, gaping hole through its starboard side. The engine room was immediately flooded, causing the engine to stop. All the engine room crew got out except one who drowned.

No distress signal could be sent because the radio room had been destroyed by the blast. The order to abandon ship was given by the captain. All of the fifty-man crew, except the one who had drowned in the engine room, were able to escape in the lifeboats and pull away from the sinking vessel. They stayed near the *Lancing* until the ship finally went down just as daylight broke. Within another few hours, they were all rescued by the tanker *Pan Rhode Island* and the HMS *Hertfordshire* and carried to Norfolk, Virginia.

Topp and the *U-552* had long since left the area and headed out to sea. He would give his crew some needed rest and then move west to Cape Lookout.

THE *ATLAS*

On the night of April 8, Topp was again close inshore near Cape Lookout and anxious to extend his list of ships sunk. He could see Cape Lookout from where he waited on the surface for any approaching ships. By mid-evening, his lookouts had one in sight coming up from the west.

The 430-foot-long tanker *Atlas* was en route from Houston, Texas, to Seawarren, New Jersey, with a load of eighty-five thousand barrels of gasoline. Captain Hamilton Gray was aware of the numerous sinkings by U-boats that had occurred over the past few weeks and made sure his ship was completely blacked out and moving along at flank speed. He had decided that while passing Cape Lookout, he would stay inside the shoals,

Atlas, sunk near Cape Lookout by *U-552*. *National Archives.*

where the ocean was less than 50 feet deep. This, he thought, would give his ship and his crew an edge over any U-boat that might be in the area.

Just before the first torpedo hit, one of the lookouts on the *Atlas* thought he heard the sound of an engine grinding in the distance. The captain ordered the ship turned with the stern facing the direction of the sound. It was too late. The torpedo crashed into the starboard side of the *Atlas*. Gasoline flowed from the ruptured tanks but didn't ignite. The captain realized that this was only temporary. He had the engines stopped and ordered the crew to take to the lifeboats.

All thirty-four crewmen were able to safely get off the ship and into the sea in three lifeboats. Knowing that the water was being covered with gasoline from the massive hole in the storage tanks, the men pulled in an attempt to put as much distance between them and the *Atlas* as possible.

Out of the darkness came the U-boat. Topp had decided to get in closer and finish the job. As the men in the lifeboats watched, another torpedo was sent into the *Atlas*. This one ignited the gasoline on the ship and in the water.

Two of the lifeboats were clear of the fire that erupted around the *Atlas*, but the one with the captain on board was not. Soon, the boat was engulfed in flames, and the eleven men jumped overboard to avoid being burned to death. After the flames burned out, they returned to the lifeboat. All but two made it.

Coast guard patrol boats picked up all thirty-two men at about seven o'clock in the morning and took them to Morehead City. They were only five miles from shore.

Topp was not through for the night. He moved away into the darkness and headed southeast, away from the Cape. He would find one more ship to sink before returning to France. It would be the *Tamaulipas*.

The *Tamaulipas*

Erich Topp was down to his last torpedo and was low on fuel. He moved southeast toward Cape Hatteras in hopes of bagging one more ship. Almost as soon as he got away from the burning *Atlas*, he spotted another tanker up ahead. It was the *Tamaulipas*.

The captain of the 435-foot-long, seven-thousand-ton *Tamaulipas* was trying to make it around Cape Hatteras by daylight. He was carrying seventy thousand barrels of oil bound for New York and wanted to get there as soon as possible. Seeing the *Atlas* burning to his northwest made the urgency all the more real. Little did he know that the U-boat that sank the *Atlas* had maneuvered ahead of him and was waiting to send his ship to the bottom, too.

Right around midnight, a torpedo hit the *Tamaulipas* on its starboard side, resulting in a terrific explosion. Within several minutes, the whole ship was aflame. Somehow, the entire thirty-seven-man crew was able to leave the ship in two lifeboats, except for two who drowned after jumping into the sea. The survivors watched as the ship appeared to break in two and sink amidships in a boiling mass of flames.

The men didn't have to wait long to be rescued. Within two hours, the armed trawler HMS *Norwich City* picked them all up and carried them to Morehead City.

Korvettenkapitan Erich Topp had fired *U-552*'s last torpedo and began the long trip back to France. Since arriving only one week earlier, he had sunk five ships with little opposition from American forces along the North Carolina coast.

The *San Delfino*

Erich Topp was gone, but several of the U-boats that left France in March were still around. One of these was the Type VIIC *U-203* and its commander, Rolf Mutzelburg. Mutzelburg left France on March 12 and had been patrolling off Hatteras for about one week. He was off Wimble Shoals just east of Rodanthe when his lookouts spotted the *San Delfino* moving north up the coast. It had made it past Cape Hatteras, and its captain, Albert Gumbleton, thought the worst was behind him. He was wrong.

The *San Delfino* was an eight-thousand-ton tanker en route from Houston, Texas, to Halifax, Nova Scotia, with eleven thousand tons of aviation fuel and an unknown amount of ammunition. The ship was well armed, was zigzagging and was blacked out as it proceeded along about ten o'clock on the night of April 9. Many of the fifty-man crew were awake when the first torpedo hit the ship on its starboard side. The ship kept going, and two more torpedoes were fired in a second attack ten minutes later. Both of these missed the ship completely.

The *San Delfino* soon was out of range, and Mutzelburg had to pull ahead of the ship and set up again for attack number three. He had used three of his fourteen torpedoes, and the *San Delfino* was still making way.

The next torpedo hit resulted in a violent explosion of both the aviation fuel and the ammunition. The ship was so engulfed in flames that the captain ordered the engines stopped and told the crew to abandon ship.

The first lifeboat down, with twenty-eight crewmen in it, was immediately drawn into the flaming aviation fuel, and its occupants were burned alive. The other boat, with twenty-two more crewmen, escaped the flames and pulled a safe distance away, where they watched the *San Delfino* burn. They remained in the area until they were picked up by a fishing trawler that had been operating nearby.

The ship continued to burn for an undetermined period before it sank in about two hundred feet of water.

THE *MALCHASE*

In the early morning darkness of April 9, the small 3,500-ton freighter *Malchase* had just passed offshore Cape Lookout. It was coming from Baton Rouge, Louisiana, and heading for Hopewell, New Jersey, with 3,600 tons of soda ash.

Captain George Lassen and his *U-160* had been patrolling on the surface between Cape Hatteras and Cape Lookout for several nights. His last sinking was the *Blanco* on April 1. His lookouts spotted the small

Malchase, sunk off Cape Lookout by *U-160*. *National Archives.*

Malchase coming up south of their position and called Lassen to the bridge of the conning tower. Seeing the ship, Lassen saw that it was not a tanker or a large freighter but decided to sink it anyway. He thought he would need only one torpedo to do it.

As the *Malchas*e passed in front of him on his seaward side, he fired a single torpedo into its port side. No one on the freighter saw it coming. The torpedo exploded with enough force to blow a large hole in the hull below the waterline, and the ship appeared to be in danger of sinking immediately. Captain Magunusbal realized this and ordered the engines stopped and told the twenty-seven-man crew to abandon ship. He could not send a distress call because the radio equipment had been destroyed.

There were two lifeboats on the *Malchase*. The port boat had been destroyed by the torpedo blast, leaving only the starboard boat for twenty-eight men. The boat could hold a maximum of twenty-five men, so the captain and two other officers decided to remain on board and try to launch a raft. The lifeboat was launched without incident, and the twenty-five crew members on board waited in the sea next to the ship.

While the captain and the two officers were preparing to launch a raft they had found, the U-boat came gliding in from the darkness. Lassen circled the *Malchase* so close that the three officers could hear the Germans talking on the conning tower. They paid no attention to any of the survivors and moved around to the port side out of sight.

The raft was launched, and the two vessels moved away from the *Malchase*. They were no more than fifty yards away when another torpedo hit the ship. An additional hole was blown in the port side, letting more sea water in and flooding the engine room. This was enough to cause the *Malchase* to settle and sink.

It was after eight o'clock the next morning when the twenty-eight survivors saw a ship approaching. It was the Mexican tanker *Fajo de Oro*. The twenty-eight men were taken aboard and carried to just inside Cape Henry, where they were transferred to a sub-chaser. From there, they were taken to Norfolk, Virginia.

The *Empire Thrush*

The morning of April 14 was a bright and clear one. The seas at Diamond Shoals buoy were light and from the northeast. One ship, the six-thousand-ton *Empire Thrush*, was moving north inside the buoy. It was en route from Tampa, Florida, to Halifax to join a convoy bound for England and was carrying, among other freight, eight hundred tons of TNT. It was zigzagging and had lookouts posted all over the ship watching for any sign of a U-boat. The ship's captain was unaware that just nine hours earlier, a German U-boat, the *U-85*, had been sunk fifteen miles east of Oregon Inlet.

The *U-85* was not the only boat operating north of Cape Hatteras. Rolf Mutzelburg and his *U-203* were waiting up ahead for the *Empire Thrush* to move into range for a submerged torpedo attack. The deck gun and machine guns aboard the *Thrush* would do the ship no good since *U-203* was submerged.

About nine o'clock, Mutzelburg fired one torpedo into the starboard side of the *Empire Thrush*. One of the men on watch saw the torpedo coming, but it was too late to do anything about it. The explosion didn't set off the TNT, but the captain, George Fisk, ordered the ship abandoned anyway, anticipating another torpedo and the explosion of the TNT.

The nice weather and the fact that it was daylight aided the evacuation from the ship, and within twenty minutes, all fifty-five crewmen were safely in lifeboats and away from the *Thrush*. They were picked up two hours later by the Q ship *Evelyn* and taken to Norfolk. The *Empire Thrush* soon sank, with its masts and funnel still above the surface.

THE BUCKET BRIGADE

By April 16, a new system of getting the tanker and freighter traffic past Cape Hatteras and other dangerous areas along the North Carolina coastline had been put into place by Admiral King and Andrews. It was called the Bucket Brigade and worked this way: ships passing along the coast would spend the night in safe ports or inshore areas and be escorted by navy and coast guard vessels from port to port during the daytime. The night havens were usually no more than 125 miles apart.

THE *DESERT LIGHT*

The *Desert Light* was proceeding from New York to Bermuda with a load of military supplies, including one hundred tons of ammunition and dynamite. On the morning of April 16, it was about one hundred miles east of Cape Hatteras. Not part of the Bucket Brigade operation, it was traveling alone.

Captain Heinz Hirsacker and *U-572* were operating on the surface and heading in toward the Cape Hatteras area when his lookouts spotted the *Desert Light*. He approached the ship and fired two torpedoes into its starboard side. The little ship, only two thousand tons, went down after about one hour. Thirty of the thirty-one crewmen escaped in one lifeboat and one raft, where they stayed for seven days before being picked up by the *Roper* on the twenty-third. They were all taken to Morehead City.

THE *EMPIRE DRYDEN*

Around the middle of April, many of the captains of the tankers and freighters that had to pass the Cape Hatteras area decided to make the passage way offshore, sometimes as far out as three hundred miles. Other ships heading for Europe or the Far East took this same route close to Bermuda. The U-boat captains soon found out about this and moved out to this new spot themselves. They were comfortable here, being so far from land and in very deep water. They sank several ships in this new hot spot in quick succession. The *Empire Dryden* was the first.

Around nine o'clock on the night of April 19, the seven-thousand-ton freighter *Empire Dryden* was heading east about three hundred miles east of

Cape Hatteras with a load of military supplies when it was torpedoed by Heinz Hirsacker in the *U-572*. Hirsacker used three torpedoes, and the ship broke up and sank in about fifteen minutes. Hirsacker circled the ship several times but did not move in close enough to question any of the crewmen. Most of the fifty-one-member crew were able to escape the ship in three lifeboats but became separated the next day. Only twenty-two survivors eventually made it to safety on May 5, when they were picked up by the *City of Birmingham* and taken to Bermuda.

The *Harpagon*

The following night, April 20, the five-thousand-ton *Harpagon* passed near the spot where the *Empire Dryden* went down. The ship, with a crew of forty-nine, had left New York on the seventeenth and was heading for Capetown, South Africa.

Around midnight, the ship was torpedoed and sunk by Heinrich Bleichroft in the *U-109*. The captain and forty of the crew were lost. Eight crew members were picked up by the Argentinian merchant ship *Rio Diamante* and landed in Buenos Aires.

The *Agra*

Less than twenty-four hours later, the four-thousand-ton freighter *Agra*, following the same route as the previous two ships, was hit by two torpedoes and sunk by Ludwig Forster in the *U-654*. It had been heading for Capetown with seven thousand tons of general cargo.

Two other U-boats, *U-136* and *U-572*, were in the same area and had chased the *Agra* right into the path of the *U-654*. They watched as Forster sunk it.

Of the thirty-nine crewmen on board, thirty-three survived and were picked up by the Norwegian ship *Tercero* and taken to Bermuda.

THE *CHENANGO*

On the night of April 20, the three-thousand-ton *Chenango* was heading for Baltimore with a load of manganese ore when it was torpedoed by Horst Uphoff in *U-84*.

The ship was about sixty miles southeast of Cape Henry when a single torpedo sent it to the bottom in less than five minutes. Of the thirty-eight crewmen onboard, only two got off and climbed onto a raft that was floating in the sea. Twelve days later, they were spotted and picked up by a seaplane. They had drifted forty miles southwest to a spot east of Oregon Inlet. One of these men later died, leaving only one survivor. The location of the sunken *Chenango* was not found until after the war.

THE *BRIS*

Around nine o'clock at night on April 20, the two-thousand-ton freighter *Bris* was hit on the port side by a torpedo fired from Adalbert Schnee's *U-201*. The ship was in the new hunting grounds about two hundred miles northwest of Bermuda and was carrying asphalt and flour from Baltimore to Natal, Brazil.

The ship sank in less than ten minutes, and all but four of the twenty-five-man crew escaped in two lifeboats. They drifted until May 3, when they were picked up just east of Cape Fear by the *Chester D. Swain* and taken to Charleston, South Carolina.

THE *ASHKHABAD*

The last ship to sink as a result of a torpedo attack off the North Carolina coast in April was the five-thousand-ton tanker *Ashkhabad*. The ship left New York bound for Cuba in ballast on April 26 and had made it as far as Cape Lookout by the night of April 30. It was a clear night with a full moon shining as the ship rounded the Cape and headed for Cape Fear. It was being escorted by the HMS *Lady Elsa*.

About 9:00 p.m., lookouts on the *Elsa* spotted a U-boat on the surface some six hundred yards north of the *Ashkhabad*. It was already too late,

Ashkhabad, sunk near Cape Lookout by *U-402*. *National Archives*.

as Siegfried von Forstner had already fired a single torpedo from his forward tubes.

The *Ashkhabad* was hit on its starboard side in the number four hold. The engines were stopped, and the ship settled stern first on the fifty-foot bottom. The bow area did not sink and remained above the surface.

In about an hour, the captain, Alexy Pavlovitch, decided to abandon ship, and the entire complement of forty-four men and three women left the still floating *Ashkhabad* in two lifeboats and a raft and were immediately picked up by the *Lady Elsa*. They were all taken to Morehead City.

The next day, the Russians decided to salvage the *Ashkhabad*, and the navy tug *Relief* headed for the still floating ship. The destroyer *Semmes* apparently didn't know this when it fired three three-inch rounds into the *Ashkhabad*, setting it on fire. Nor did the HMS *St. Zeno* when this ship fired another shell into the burning *Ashkhabad*. No salvage attempt was made, as the ship was now a total loss.

Back in Germany, Admiral Karl Donitz wrote the following in his official BdU war diary concerning American operations during the month of April:

Attacking conditions in the American area continue to be very good. Anti-submarine activity has increased, but its fighting power, its concentration, and its determination to attack and destroy are small. Those who fight are not sailors, but people who are being paid for their presence in the area endangered by U-boats. Commanding officers are all of the same opinion, namely that the American area will remain a highly favorable area for attacks for some months to come and that a high percentage of successes can be scored with very few losses.

By the end of April, Admiral Andrews had his own ideas about the German U-boat menace and what he needed to do about it. It had become evident to him that two things must be done immediately. He went to Admiral King and told him the following: something had to be done immediately to stop the tanker losses along the East Coast of the United States, and a convoy system of ships and escorts had to be implemented now.

The order soon went out that all commercial oil tankers were to be held in port until further orders were given and that all U.S. tankers were to immediately be placed under the control of Admiral Andrews. Andrews knew that the only answer was convoying with adequate escorts and that this would take some time. The Bucket Brigade system was a good start, but it was not enough to solve the problem.

CHAPTER 9

THE *U-85*

The *U-85* was the first U-boat to be sunk by an American surface vessel in World War II. This happened in the early morning hours of April 14 about fifteen miles east of Nags Head. It was caught on the surface by the destroyer USS *Roper* and sent to the bottom with all hands. This is the saga of that boat and how it came to end up that night on the sandy bottom. It is an important event in North Carolina coastal history.

THE BOAT

At the beginning of World War II, Germany had fewer than thirty operational U-boats in service. The conceptual use for these boats ranged from mine laying and reconnaissance to an all-out war on shipping. The larger boats of the IXC class were preferred by the naval leadership as strategic weapons, while the smaller and more maneuverable Class VII boats like the *U-85* were used to wage the convoy battles of the North Atlantic.

All of these U-boats were essentially surface craft with the capability of staying submerged only for very short periods of time. They all relied on diesel engines for surface propulsion and electric motors for running submerged. The electric motors were powered by storage batteries carried below the U-boats' flooring. These batteries required daily recharging by the diesel engines, which could only be done when the boat was surfaced.

U-85 (outside) and *U-751* dock at St. Nazaire on February 23, 1942. *Bundesarchiv, Koblenz.*

U-85 enters St. Nazaire U-boat pens behind *U-751*. *Bundesarchiv, Koblenz.*

TYPE VIIB

U-85, a member of the second generation of Class Type VII U-boats, was one of 24 submarines built and designated by design characteristics as a Type VIIB. The type VII boat, of which 709 were built in Germany between 1936 and 1945, was the workhorse of the Kreigsmarine undersea fleet during the Second World War. The majority of Type VII boats were Type VIICs and included 600 submarines. Of the 1,152 boats built by Germany between 1936 and 1945, the majority were Type VIIs.

The Type VIIB, outclassing its VIIA predecessor with improved speed, range and weaponry, became in early 1938 the preferred operational U-boat of the commander in chief of submarines, BdU Karl Donitz. Had it not been for several technical developments in sensor equipment and the need for more hull space, the VIIB would have been Germany's most produced U-boat of the war.

The first Type VIIB, *U-45*, was commissioned on June 25, 1938, and the last one, *U-87*, on August 19, 1941. Of the VIIB boats, *U-45* to *U-55* and

Type VIIB Internal Profile and Plan

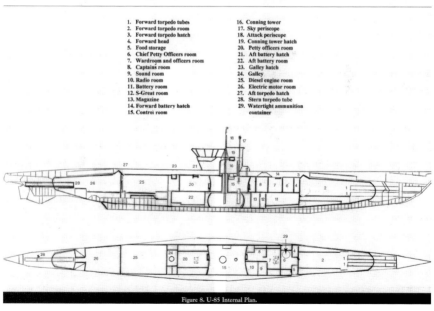

1. Forward torpedo tubes	16. Conning tower
2. Forward torpedo room	17. Sky periscope
3. Forward torpedo hatch	18. Attack periscope
4. Forward head	19. Conning tower hatch
5. Food storage	20. Petty officers room
6. Chief Petty Officers room	21. Aft battery hatch
7. Wardroom and officers room	22. Aft battery room
8. Captains room	23. Galley hatch
9. Sound room	24. Galley
10. Radio room	25. Diesel engine room
11. Battery room	26. Electric motor room
12. S-Great room	27. Aft torpedo hatch
13. Magazine	28. Stern torpedo tube
14. Forward battery hatch	29. Watertight ammunition
15. Control room	container

Figure 8. U-85 Internal Plan.

Diagram of Type VIIB U-boat. *Jim Bunch.*

German Type VIIB Submarine
24 constructed between 1936 and 1940

U-boat	Builder	Work #	Built
U-45 - U-50	Germaniawerft AG, Kiel	580-585	1936-1937
U-51 - U-55	Germaniawerft AG, Kiel	586-590	1938-1939
U-73 U-76	Vegesacker Werft, Vegesack	1-4	1938-1940
U-83 U-87	Flender-Werke AG, Lubeck	291, 280-283	1938-1941
U-99 U-102	Germaniawerft AG, Kiel	593-596	1937-1940

Technical Specifications

Displacement:	704 (d)	Speed:	17.9 (sf)
(tons)	753 (sf)	(knots)	8.0 (sm)
	857 (sm)		
	1040 (total)	Range	8700/10 (sf)
		(miles/knots)	90/4 (sm)
Length: (m)	66.5 oa		
	48.8 ph	Torpedoes:	14
Beam: (m)	6.2 oa	Mines:	39 TMB
	4.7ph		
		Deck Gun:	8.8cm
			C35L/45
Draught: (m)	4.75		220 rounds
Height: (m)	9.5	AA Gun	2cm C30
Power: (hp)	3200 (sf)	Crew	44-48 men
	750 (sm)		
		Max. Depth:	725 feet

sm = submerged, sf = surfaced oa = overall
ph = pressure hull, hp = horsepower

Technical specifications for Type VII U-boat. *Jim Bunch.*

U-99 to *U-102* were built at the Germania Shipyards in Kiel, *U-73* to *U-76* at Bremer Vulcan in Vegesack and *U-83* to *U-87* at Flender Werft in Lubeck.

Type VIIBs included Otto Kretschmer's famous *U-99*, Gunther Prien's *U-47*, Schepke's *U-100* and Bleichrodt's *U-48*, the most successful U-boat of the war, sinking fifty-three ships. By 1945, only the *U-46*, *U-48*, *U-52* and *U-78* were still afloat. Their own crews scuttled them that year.

At war's end, the entire group of twenty-four VIIBs had sunk more than 250 ships.

U-85 CONSTRUCTION DETAILS

The "K" Office of the Oberkomando der Kriegsmarine contracted *U-85* and seven other VIIBs on June 9, 1938. The order number was 291-280-283, and the building yard chosen was Flender-Werke AG. The keel was laid on December 18, 1939, and the boat launched on April 10, 1941. Commissioning by Oberleutnant Eberhard Gerger took place on June 7, 1941. The boat was given a feldpost number of M40935. Every German naval unit had its own feldpost number. The number, used primarily as a postal address, was also used as a security device to recall a U-boat crew from a public place.

U-85 was a single-hull design, the pressure hull also being the outer hull. The hull was fabricated from steel and ranged in thickness from 0.75 inches to 0.65 inches and was reinforced with strengthening ribs every 24 inches. The weakest point was where the conning tower was attached; it was 0.88 inches thick here.

The pressure hull was fabricated from eight steel modules that were built separately and welded together. A large hole in the top of module five, located next to the aftermost module, was left open as an access point to outfit and equip the U-boat.

After all items, including the diesel engines and electric motors, were loaded inside, module five was sealed and the conning tower pressure hull welded in place. The superstructure, extending from the bow to the stern, was now welded on. The saddle tanks and deck armaments were added last.

When completed, *U-85* was 218 feet long and had a 160-foot pressure hull. It had a 20-foot beam, keel-to-bridge height of 31 feet and a 15.5-foot draft. The boat displaced 753 tons with the fuel and water tanks full and 1,040 tons when fully loaded and submerged. Two diesels with superchargers provided

The author under the bow of the *U-995*. *Author's collection.*

surface power of 3,200 horsepower and a maximum speed of twenty miles per hour. Two electric motors provided 750 horsepower and a submerged running speed of ten miles per hour. The two propulsion systems together enabled *U-85* to travel up to ten thousand miles without refueling.

The *U-85* was armed with four bow and one stern torpedo tubes. As an improvement over the original Type VII, the stern tube was relocated within the casing and was reloadable from the aft torpedo compartment. The boat's two rudders, an improvement from the single rudder found on Type VIIs, allowed torpedoes fired from the stern tube to pass between them. Additional storage outside the pressure hull and under the stern torpedo compartment flooring made it possible to increase the torpedo load from eleven to fourteen. One 88mm C35 L/45 gun fitted forward of the conning tower and one 20mm C30 flak gun aft of the tower gave *U-85* the weaponry to fight on and below the surface.

Inside the pressure hull, above the flooring, the boat had the following compartments: forward torpedo room and crew's quarters, officer and chief mates' quarters, control room with attack center (conning tower) above,

Above: *U-85* arrives in St. Nazaire on February 23, 1942, following its third war cruise. Note the two victory pennants on the flagpole behind Obersteurman Wendt. Greger mistakenly thought he had sunk the nine-thousand-ton merchantman *Port Wyndham*. He did sink the *Empire Fusselier*, indicated by the six-thousand-ton pennant. *Bundesarchiv, Koblenz.*

Right: *U-85* crew member Willy Matthies stands by the U-boat's deck gun. *Bundesarchiv, Koblenz.*

Greger and Obersteuermann Heinz Wendt bring *U-85* alongside the dock at St. Nazare. *Bundesarchiv, Koblenz.*

senior rates quarters and galley, diesel engine room, electric motor room and after-torpedo compartment.

The forward torpedo room was thirty-six feet long and had space for ten torpedoes, twelve bunks and twenty-four enlisted men. The officer and chief mates' quarters were aft of the forward torpedo room and accommodated five officers, including the captain and four chief petty officers. This space was twenty-four feet long and separated from the forward area by a thin metal wall and rectangular doorway. The radio and sound rooms were located on the starboard side of this compartment adjacent to the control room. Next came the twenty-foot-long control room, accessible on both ends by round watertight hatches. Above the control room, another watertight round hatch led to the attack center. Behind the control room, the senior rates quarters and galley consumed another twenty-two feet of pressure hull and included eight bunks for sixteen men to eat and sleep. The twenty-four-foot-long diesel engine room with its narrow hallway between the two MAN diesel engines came next, located behind a thin metal wall and a rectangular door. The aft-room was the electric motor and stern torpedo room. This thirty-four-foot-long room held the two electric motors for submerged running and the stern torpedo tube. No men slept in this compartment.

The author by the torpedo tubes in the forward torpedo room of *U-995*. *Author's collection.*

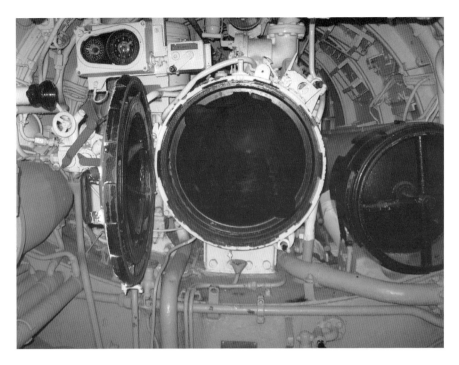

U-995, stern torpedo tube in stern torpedo room. *Author's collection.*

The area below the deck plating in the officers' quarters, senior rates quarters and control room was almost as large as the living and working space above. Here were found the battery rooms and the 125 batteries, the 256-cubic-foot magazine, fuel and freshwater tanks, main diving tanks and the S-Gerat (sound detection equipment) compartment. The forward trim tank, torpedo compensating tanks and storage space for four reserve torpedoes were below the forward torpedo room and crew's quarters. The aft trim tank, torpedo compensating tank and storage space for one torpedo were located below the stern torpedo-loading compartment.

The Crew

All U-boat men were supposedly volunteers, but this was not always the case. Any person judged fit for U-boat service was required to volunteer for it. Forty-six men made up the crew of *U-85*. Whether they were all volunteers

U-85 crew members are greeted by KK Sohler, chief of the Seventh U-boat Flotilla, after docking at St. Nazaire on February 23, 1942. *Bundesarchiv, Koblenz.*

is unknown. They did range in age from nineteen to thirty-six and were divided by rank and number into three groups composed of officers, noncommissioned officers and enlisted men. The noncommissioned officers were warrant, chief petty and petty officers. Each man, except for the officers, functioned as either a seaman or a member of the technical division. The night *U-85* was sunk, there were five officers, six senior noncommissioned officers, eleven petty officers and twenty-four enlisted men on board. This group of men was the last crew but not the starting crew from 1941. Many of the original crew members had gone on to other assignments, mostly after the third cruise.

OFFICERS

The commanding officer on *U-85* was Captain Oberleutnant zur See Eberhard Greger. Greger, a member of crew 35, was twenty-seven years old and a graduate of the Marineschule Murwik in Flensburg, where he was commissioned an oberleutnant zur see on October 1, 1939. Unlike their

Annapolis counterparts, German naval officers were designated by the year they entered the naval academy rather than when they graduated. Forty-five U-boat commanders emerged from the crew of 1935.

Before taking command of the *U-85*, Greger had gained experience as the second watch officer aboard the destroyer *Wolfgang Zenker* and the first watch officer under the command of Fritz Julius Lemp aboard the *U-30* and *U-110*. Lemp mistakenly sank the passenger liner *Athenia* several days after the beginning of the Second World War and on May 9, 1941, allowed the *U-110* and its three-rotor Enigma machine to be captured on the surface. On the morning of the tenth, *U-110* sank while under tow by the HMS *Bulldog*.

Greger commissioned and commanded the *85* from its launching on June 7, 1941, until it was sunk in April 1942.

With two years of combat experience behind him, Greger was an able commanding officer with a seasoned crew. On him, as with all U-boat commanders, was placed the ultimate responsibility for the U-boat's success or failure. Of his many duties, one was to supervise the first watch officer during surface torpedo attacks. Having been the first watch officer on the *U-30* and the *U-110*, he was very experienced in surface engagements and

Greger and Sohler talk with *U-85*'s officers on the deck of *U-85* following the boat's return from its third war cruise. *Bundesarchiv, Koblenz.*

Oberleutnant zur See Eberhard Greger, captain of the *U-85*, talks with an officer from the *U-751* on the docks at St. Nazaire, France. *Bundesarchiv, Koblenz.*

U-boat captain Gerhard Bigalk and Greger. *Author's collection.*

responsible for several sinkings. He was on the bridge doing this the night *U-85* was sunk by the *Roper*.

As kommandant, he had his own private quarters adjacent to the control room. The radio and sound rooms were only a few feet from his bunk. He spent most of his time in the control room, on the bridge or in the conning tower behind the attack periscope.

Four other officers—Oberleutnant zur See Kurt Fraesdorff, Oberleutnant Helmut Lechler, Oberleutnant Ingenieur Hans Sanger and Leutnant Wolfgang Komorowski—were the other senior officers on board the *U-85* and had various responsibilities. Their bunks were in the compartment adjacent to the captain's quarters and just forward of the sound room. A permanent mess table here was used by the four officers and the captain as a wardroom and discussion center.

Twenty-four-year old Lechler, the first watch officer, was the second most important man on the boat and took command in the event that something incapacitated the captain. He was responsible for the readiness of the boat's torpedoes and conducted surface torpedo attacks. He also supervised and organized the first bridge watch. He fired the one torpedo that barely missed the *Roper* on the night of April 14.

Captain Greger talks with an officer from the *U-751* on the docks at St. Nazaire. The other two men in hats are probably agents sent by the State Security Office in Berlin. *Bundesarchiv, Koblenz.*

The officers of *U-85* in front of the conning tower at Flenderwerft shipyard in Lubeck, just after the U-boat was completed. *From left to right*: Oberleutnant zur See Helmut Lechler, Oberleutnant zur See Hans Sanger, Oberleutnant zur See Eberhard Greger and Leutnant zur See Wolfgang Komorowski. *Matthias Vogt.*

Left: Oberleutnant Helmut Lechter was the first watch officer on the *U-85*. *Matthias Vogt*.

Right: Oberleutnant zur See Hans Sanger was the LI, or chief engineer, on the *U-85*. He was the only officer whose body was recovered after the sinking of the *U-85*. *Ed Caram*.

The second watch officer, twenty-four-year old Wolfgang Komorowski, had responsibility for the U-boat's deck guns, provisions and communications systems. He was in charge of the Enigma machine and encrypted secret radio messages when necessary. The second bridge watch was his responsibility. On April 14, he was busy directing the planned use of *U-85*'s 88mm deck gun and 20 mm flak gun against the *Roper*.

Twenty-five-year-old Hans Sanger, the chief engineer, or LI, was responsible for the technical operation of *U-85*. All physical systems on the boat fell under his control. He kept the captain advised on all technical matters affecting the boat. He was, in many respects, another captain. Most of his time was spent in the control room working with the captain. He had no specific watch but was on constant call. He maintained the diving data log and his own war diary for the operation of the vessel's engines. He was at his station behind the two plainsmen in the control room during the battle of April 14. He eventually abandoned ship and was the only officer recovered from the sea by the *Roper*.

The fourth officer, twenty-seven-year-old Kurt Fraesdorff, was a commander in training. He was on board to observe an operational U-boat and learn what he could from its officers and men. He probably would have been promoted to a U-boat commander before his next patrol.

CHIEF PETTY OFFICERS

The six chief petty officers had responsibilities almost equal to those of the senior officers. The four most senior of these men shared a compartment aft of the bow torpedo room and adjacent to the officers' quarters. They ate and slept here but spent most of their time in different areas of the boat.

Most senior of these was Obersteuermann Heinz Wendt. Wendt, the twenty-eight-year-old chief helmsman and navigator, was responsible for navigational and provisional matters aboard the U-boat. He had direct authority over the boat's helmsman and was in charge of plotting and recording the boat's course. Wendt also acted as third watch officer.

The net senior CPO was twenty-five-year-old Oberbootsmannsmatt Oskar Prantl. Also referred to as number one, he was responsible for the conduct of the seaman's division of the crew. It was his job to see that each man's clothing and equipment was in order. He also tried to settle disputes among the seamen before the problems reached the captain. He also was responsible for the cleaning of the vessel and the fourth watch. Prantl was probably with the captain on the bridge of the conning tower entering data into the torpedo attack calculator just before the *U-85* went down.

All ammunition and small arms stored aboard the U-boat were accountable to Prantl's first mate, Bootsmannsmatt Helmut Kaiser. Referred to as number two, Kaiser was required to sign off for all of the above items when checked out or used by the crew. Prantl's third mate, Bootsmannsmatt Willy Matthies, was responsible for the final cleanup when the boat returned to base.

The two remaining senior CPOs, Stabsobermachinist Eugen Ungethuem and Obermachinist Heinrich Adrian, were responsible for the diesel engines and electric motors that powered the U-boat. They reported directly to the LI, Hans Sanger. They also had responsibility or supervision of the technical division of the crew. CPO Obermachinist Fredrich Strobel served under these two men.

The last CPO, Oberfunkmatt Martin Wittmann, was responsible for the radio and sound rooms and the sending and receiving of messages around the clock. The Enigma machine and its operation were under his care. Petty Officer Funkmat Konstant Weidmann and enlisted men Funkoobergefreiter Hans Wobst and Funkggefreiter Heinz Waschmann paired together with Wittmann to carry out the six four-hour watch periods every twenty-four hours. These four men also had the more pleasant duty of playing the boat's collection of phonograph records.

Petty Officers and Enlisted Men

Eleven petty officers and twenty-four enlisted men made up this group. They composed the technical and seaman's divisions and did most of the work on the boat. The technical group included the torpedo men, motormen, electricians, radiomen and diesel men. The men classified as seamen were stewards, laborers, watchmen and the cook.

The petty officers lived in the compartment aft of the control room, the enlisted men in the forward torpedo room. One petty officer, the leading torpedoman Mechanikermatt Oskar Hansen, slept in the forward torpedo room, keeping a close maintenance check on the torpedoes.

Captain Greger salutes the U-boat flotilla commander after returning from his second war cruise. It's interesting to note that he uses the military, not the Nazi, salute. *Matthias Vogt.*

The entire complement was lost as a result of the battle that took place on April 14, 1942. Machine gun fire and an onboard explosion of one three-inch shell fired from the *Roper* killed some. After abandoning ship, most died in the water from internal injuries caused by exploding depth charges dropped by the *Roper*.

U-85 Enters World War II

U-85 officially entered the service of the Kriegsmarine on June 7, 1941, when its captain, Oberleutnant Eberhard Greger, commissioned it. Next, hull and engine trials at Kiel under the U-Boat Acceptance Command and handling trials under the Technical Training Group for front line U-boats consumed most of the summer months of 1941. Finally, tactical convoy and attack exercises conducted off Pillau in the Baltic were successfully completed and the boat was declared FRONTREIF, or fit to sail on operational cruises.

Additional information about *U-85*'s activities during the summer of 1941 is revealed in a diary kept by Stabsobermachiist Eugen Ungethum. The diary was found floating in the sea near the spot where *U-85* went down. In his diary, Ungethum records that on July 26, the *U-85* got underway for Norway, possibly from Lubeck, at five o'clock in the morning. On the following day, twenty-two hours later, the boat tied up alongside the Blucher Bridge at Horton. Liberty was granted to part of the crew on July 30 and 31 to visit Oslo.

The boat left Horton on August 6 at six o'clock in the afternoon in a convoy for Trondheim by way of Christiansen, Scavenger, Moldjne and Aalesund. Arriving in Lofjord on August 10, it tied up alongside the *Hertha*, a depot ship for U-boats.

From Monday, August 11, to Thursday, August 28, *U-85* held firing practice in Trondheimfjord. On the morning of the thirteenth, it was rammed in forty-five feet of water by the small destroyer *T-151*, damaging its number one diving tank and steering gear.

U-85 was painted, given a final overhaul in dry dock and assigned to the third U-boat flotilla as a front boat on September 1, 1941. An emblem—a wild boar with a rose in its mouth—emulating Captain Eberhard Greger was painted on the conning tower. The German translation of boar is *eber*, meaning strong like a boar.

According to Wolfgang Klue, Lothar-Guenther Buchheim, then a marine painter and who later wrote the story of Wolfgang Peterson's film

Das Boot, painted the picture on the tower during the summer of 1941. A rose was added to the emblem in the fall when the hometown of Captain Greger became the sponsor of *U-85*. Greger's hometown was Lieberose, meaning love rose.

War Cruises

U-85 made four war cruises between August 28 and April 14 when the boat was sunk. It sank one ship, the 4,700-ton freighter SS *Thistleglen*, off the coast of Greenland on its first and none on its second. On the boat's third cruise, Greger sank the 5,400-ton freighter *Empire Fusselier* with a spread of three torpedoes. This time, he was in American waters just south of Cape Race.

Fourth War Cruise

Leaving St. Nazaire on March 21, *U-85* began its fourth and final war cruise bound for the East Coast of the United States. On board, Greger carried two recently updated versions of the three-wheel Enigma machine, designated Schlussel M by the Kriegsmarine. These new four-rotor machines that had been in service since February would cause a virtual intelligence blackout for Bletchley Park and allow *U-85* to proceed into the Atlantic undetected.

To avoid being spotted by British search planes and destroyers operating in and over the Bay of Biscay, the boat traveled submerged during daylight hours for the first three days out. On the fourth day, Greger decided that it was safe to proceed on the surface.

Crew members of the *U-85* repair damage to the stern decking sustained by a depth charge attack during their first war cruise off Greenland. The damage was extensive enough that it caused Captain Greger to return to base. *Bundesarchiv, Koblenz.*

Captain Greger receives flowers after returning from his second war cruise. *Matthias Vogt.*

U-boat pens at St. Nazaire. *Wolfgang Klue.*

For the next week, the sea was as smooth as a tabletop, and the crew enjoyed fine weather, often sunning themselves on the deck.

By the twenty-ninth, the wind had risen to gale force and heavy seas caused the torpedoes to shift inside the U-boat. The men also learned that their base at St. Nazaire had been attacked by British commandos and heavily damaged. On the thirtieth, the constant rolling in the heavy swells damaged the electric motors.

Finally, on the thirty-first, the storm broke and tranquil weather returned. For the next week, the men were able to enjoy the calm seas and warm sunshine.

On April 7, Greger approached his assigned station near the coast of the United States east of New York. He announced to the crew that the boat was about 300 nautical miles from land and 660 nautical miles from Washington, D.C.

Cruising south on the surface the night of April 9, a blinking buoy spotted by the lookouts caused an alarm to be sounded and the U-boat's crew brought to battle stations. No ships were sighted, and no action occurred.

The following night, the lookouts spotted more lights. Greger had found his first target. It was a small freighter running south through the calm seas.

Greger fired two torpedoes, sinking it with two hits. The ship was the five-thousand-ton Swedish freighter *Christina Knudsen* en route to New Orleans.

Still moving south for the next three days, the U-boat lay on the sandy bottom during daylight hours and surfaced at night to search for shipping.

By the evening of April 13, *U-85* was east of Hampton Roads and the Chesapeake Bay. Running on the surface and still moving south over very calm seas, the boat reached a position about fifteen miles northeast of Oregon Inlet near midnight. Unknown to Greger, the United States Navy destroyer *Roper* was only a few miles behind him on anti-submarine patrol and slowly closing on his position. Just after midnight, the two warships would meet.

> *The submarine war is in a way like big game hunting, but within seconds the hunter becomes the hunted and has to run for his life. Being hunted requires what I call second-stage thinking, calculating what your opponent thinks you will do and then doing the opposite. Sometimes it is like a game of chess, especially if your opponent has experience and knows the rules of the game. The stakes are high, of course.*
> —*Jurgen Oesten, commander of* U-61, U-106 *and* U-861

THE USS *ROPER*

Captain Hamilton Howe, the commander of the destroyer USS *Roper* (DD147), was quickly learning the rules of big game hunting. His ship was one of seven destroyers that had been released for convoy duty and had already seen action. His ship was nearby the night its companion destroyer *Jacob Jones* was sunk without warning by two German torpedoes from the *U-578* in the early morning hours of February 28. The captain of the *Jones* had been a good friend of Howe's, and he was anxious to sink a U-boat for his lost friend Captain Black.

The *Roper* was an old "four-pipe" destroyer launched in August 1918. It was 315 feet long and had a displacement of 1,600 tons. The ship had a 115-man crew and was armed with five three-inch guns, four .50-caliber machine guns, six torpedoes, two racks of depth charges and Y and K guns for propelling the charges over a wide area. It had a top speed of twenty-eight knots, enabling it to outrun a U-boat traveling all out at nineteen knots on the surface. It was also equipped with radar, a piece of equipment that the *Jacob Jones* did not have and of which the *U-85*'s captain was unaware.

USS *Roper* was a four-stack World War I destroyer that chased down and sank the *U-85*. *Bill Hughes.*

On the night of April 13, *Roper* steamed away from the naval base at Norfolk, Virginia, and headed out into the Atlantic on anti-submarine patrol. The ship was under the command of Lieutenant Commander Hamilton W. Howe, a 1926 graduate of the Naval Academy and a close friend of Commander David Black. Black had been killed along with most of his men when his ship, the *Jacob Jones*, was sunk. Commander Stanley C. Norton, commander of Destroyer Division 54, of which the *Roper* was flagship, was also on board.

It was a clear, cold night with calm winds when the *Roper* cleared Hampton Roads and motored southeast, parallel to the Virginia–North Carolina shoreline. Around eleven o'clock, Commander Howe decided to turn in and let the officer of the deck, Kenneth Tebo, take command of the vessel. Tebo continued along uneventfully, zigzagging on a southerly course for the next hour or so, and most of the *Roper*'s crew who were not on watch turned in for the night. The sky was beautiful and full of stars, and the calm sea glowed with phosphorescence as the *Roper*'s hull cut through it. As midnight passed, the lookouts could see Bodie Island Light and the number eight Bodie Island lighted buoy off to the southwest.

This tranquil evening was about to change.

APRIL 14, 1942

Roper's first radar contact with *U-85* came at six minutes after midnight, when the submarine was about three thousand yards away. The *Roper* was making eighteen knots and was on a course of 182 degrees true. Soon after the radar contact was made, Seaman Black, the destroyer's sonar operator, began to hear *U-85*'s high-velocity propeller noise and computed a range and bearing identical to those observed by the radar operator Ensign Jim Mouquin.

Howe was awakened and advised of the situation. He doubted that the contact was anything more than a fishing or coast guard patrol boat but decided to let Tebo pursue it anyway for practice.

As the distance between the two vessels narrowed to less than 2,100 yards, a small silhouette and wake were seen by the lookouts on the bridge of the *Roper*. The unknown vessel appeared to be running away at high speed. The wake suddenly turned sharply to port and then starboard. At this point, Tebo was convinced that the unidentified vessel was a U-boat and increased the destroyer's speed to twenty knots. He also knew that German submarines had stern tubes and ordered the helmsman to move starboard of the contact's wake and out of the direct line of a possible torpedo. By this time, Commander Howe and Commander Norton were on the bridge and following the action. Howe still did not order General Quarters. As time passed, the destroyer slowly closed on the still unidentified vessel.

When the range was reduced to about seven hundred yards, the track of a three-thousand-pound torpedo fired from *U-85*'s stern tube passed close to the port side of the destroyer. Howe now ordered General Quarters, and the *Roper*'s crew began readying themselves and the ship for a fight. Tebo, still in charge of the bridge, increased speed again and continued the chase. As the range continued to decrease, *Roper*'s twenty-four-inch searchlight was switched on and the *U-85* was finally seen about three hundred yards ahead, turning to starboard.

Realizing that he had been found, Greger continued to turn *U-85* to starboard inside the turning circle of the destroyer. He may have been trying to maneuver into position for a bow torpedo shot, but it was too late for that now.

The water here was only one hundred feet deep. Greger had to either scuttle and surrender or fight it out on the surface. He chose to fight. The 88mm gun crew poured out of the conning tower and headed for their deck gun.

On the destroyer, Chief Boatswain's Mate Jack Right opened fire with his .50-caliber machine gun, raking the U-boat with tracers and preventing the gun crew from reaching their 88mm deck gun. The other three heavy machine guns on the *Roper* either jammed or misfired and could not be brought into action.

As the U-boat continued to turn, *Roper*'s searchlight illuminated several crewmen jumping from the submarine into the sea while others desperately tried to man the deck gun. Wright continued fire, keeping most of the sub's crew pinned behind the conning tower.

Minutes later, when the two vessels were side to side and only several hundred yards apart, *U-85* slowed and stopped dead in the water. The *Roper* also slowed to keep the U-boat in sight as Harry Heyman and his gun crew readied their number five three-inch gun. Heyman, the gun captain, yelled "fire," and an armor-piercing shell was sent screaming toward the *U-85*. A moment later, an orange flash was seen on the aft end of the sub's conning tower by the *Roper*'s crew. While Wright and Heyman continued to fire, a steady stream of Germans squeezed out of their conning tower hatch and jumped into the ocean.

As *U-85* now sank slowly stern first, the executive officer on the *Roper*, Lieutenant Vancus, wrote in his post-sinking report that he saw about thirty-five men in the water. Commander Howe also noted in his report that "about forty of the U-boat's crew were sighted in the sea." Whether the direct hit by Harry Heyman's number five gun or an order from Greger to scuttle and abandon ship caused the *U-85* to sink is still unknown.

Although the blast from the three-inch shell penetrated the pressure hull above the control room and caused flooding, the penetration was small and probably could not have caused the U-boat to sink as fast as it did. This was confirmed by Rhodes Chamberlin in an interview with the author. He explained how the boat sank in a matter of minutes, stern first. This would suggest that *U-85* was scuttled by opening the stern torpedo door.

Sensing that the sub was finished, Captain Greger most likely ordered the boat scuttled as the crew scrambled to exit the boat. What happened to Greger is still a mystery.

As *U-85*'s deck disappeared beneath the surface of the ocean, most of the crew had already jumped into the near freezing water. The *Roper*, now less than one hundred yards from the spot where *U-85* sank, powered ahead through a sea of German sailors, all wearing life vests and calling for help. A life raft was ordered dropped from the *Roper*, but it became fouled in the rigging. Before the destroyer could circle again, a sonar contact prompted

Commander Howe to decide not to stop and attempt a rescue. Another U-boat could be nearby, ready to sink the stopped destroyer. The *Jacob Jones* disaster was still fresh in Howe's memory, and he had his own ship and men to think about. Instead of dropping a life raft, a pattern of eleven depth charges was sent flying from the Y and K guns toward the spot where *U-85* went down. The five-hundred-pound depth charges were set to explode at fifty feet and killed all the survivors in the water

The destroyer circled again and then slowed and turned off the searchlight. For the rest of the night, *Roper* remained in the area, searching and listening. Commander Norton returned to his cabin and wrote his report. The men of the *Roper* had made the first American U-boat kill of World War II by an American warship.

The following morning, two planes and a blimp arrived from the coast guard base near Elizabeth City and dropped smoke flares near a large oil slick rising from the *U-85*. Many bodies and debris were spotted floating in

Commander Howe (*left*) and Commander Norton prepare their reports on board the *Roper* following the sinking of *U-85*. *National Archives.*

Diary of Erich Degenkolb

A crewman aboard U-85 when it was sunk.

Calendar for year 1942.
Inscription: Fortune favors the efficient in the long run.

Jan. 1) Hilgegard Anhut U-boat home Lorient   Organization Todt-
          good evening of dancing.
      2) Nothing special   a lot of work.
      3) Good orchestra   U-boat home.
      4) Same.
      5) Clean ship at sea.
      6) Letter from home.
     10) We sail.
     11) A/C alarm   getting warmer. Seasick   Oh Neptune.
     12) Badly seasick.
     13) No end to it.
     14) Sanchan Sorensen's birthday 1925.
     15) Slowly getting better.
     16) Good weather.
     17) All up and well.
     18) First steamer sighted   got away.
     19) Horrible seas.
     20) Food tastes good again.
     21) Evening 7.35   a 10,000 ton ship sunk with a fan of four.
     22) Action stations early   Steamer escapes at full speed.
     23) 4/5 speed after it   couldn't catch it.
     24) Calm weather   11.00 in evening action stations. My beard is
          growing noticeably. The first German U-boats off the
          American coast.
     25) Quiet day.
     26) It is getting much cooler.
     27) Baptism of fire   A/C attack.
     28) Below Zero.
     29) Abominably cold   hardly bearable.
     30) Hitler speaks   off Newfoundland.
     31) Heavy seas   barometer rising and falling   we are off New York.

Feb. 1) 10,000 ton tanker sighted - ran away from us.
      2) Good weather - quiet day - 24.30 hurra! for home.
      3) Sea quite flat - took pictures.
     23) We reach home after successful cruise.

March 1) On leave.
      14) Back again.
      21) 18.00 we leave from St. Nazaire.
      22) We cruise submerged   in the distance depth charges.
      23) Submerged   quiet.
      24) We cruise on surface   magnificent weather.
      25) Sea as smooth as a table.
      26) Magnificent sunrise.
      27) The wind comes up   seasickness easy to find.
      28) Barometer rising   special announcement   landing at St. Nazaire.
      29) Torpedoes shift in heavy seas and beautiful music. Special
           announcement   116,000 tons sunk.
      30) Cut in electric motors   heavy seas   sighted whales.
      31) Quiet weather   nothing important.

April 1) Crashes. Inclination 55° St. B. or bearing 55° St. B.
       2) Changeable weather   rain.
       3) Light swell   magnificent sunshine.
       4) We aim torpedoes   cold   sea smooth big cake   baking.
           Abominable heat in the Gulf Stream.
       5) Noon   magnificent sunshine just off America. Thoughts of home.
       6) Night sky   still day light.
       7) 300 nautical miles from land.   660 to Washington.
       8) Abominable heat. All stripped bare.
       9) Alarm - before a buoy. 6 above zero.
      10) A steamer sighted and sunk 0100. fan of 2   2 hits.
      11) 1240   50 meters depth. Off Washington - We cruise submerged.
           1830 - 8.5 meters under keel. 3 weeks at sea   3 steamers heard.
      12) We lie on bottom all day. All is asleep off New York.
      13) American beacons and searchlights visible at night.

Diary of a *U-85* crewman. *Jim Bunch.*

Left: Tombstone of Erich Degenkolb, a member of the crew of the *U-85*. Twenty-nine crew members are buried in Hampton National Cemetery. *Author's collection.*

Below: Crew members of the *U-85* recovered from the sea are transferred from the *Roper* to the tug *Sciota* in Hampton Roads for transport to the Norfolk Naval Base. *National Archives.*

the water. At one time, at least seven planes and a blimp circled the area. The *Roper* dropped six more depth charges over the oil slick before stopping near the floats to pick up the bodies and other debris from the sunken U-boat.

Twenty-nine dead sailors were recovered, but Captain Greger was not among them. Two bodies were so badly damaged that they were allowed to sink after being searched.

Diaries kept by seamen Eric Degenkolb and Eugen Ungethum were also found in the sea, revealing much about life on the *U-85* and its four war cruises.

After dropping a large orange buoy near the spot where *U-85* went down, the *Roper* returned to Norfolk and the bodies and diaries were turned over to naval intelligence. Several days later, the twenty-nine dead German sailors were buried at Hampton National Cemetery near Newport News, Virginia.

What happened to the fifteen U-boat crewmen not accounted for? No human remains have ever been found on the *U-85*. Stories of German U-boat men reaching the coast in rubber rafts soon after the sinking have never been disproved. Did some of *U-85*'s crew escape and reach the mainland? Probably not. Commander Howe said he saw "about forty men" in the water as the U-boat went down. The rest were most likely killed by machine gun fire and fell into the sea.

Rhodes Chamberlin

Rhodes Chamberlin was the seaman on the *Roper* who was supposed to release the raft for the German survivors to climb into after their U-boat went down. This is his testimonial of what really happened that night. He presented this author with a letter, written on February 14, 2001, containing his recollections of the night of April 13 through April 14, 1942:

It's April 13, 1942—the start of another week or so of antisubmarine patrol off Cape Hatteras. That evening I had the 8–12 watch in the Radio shack and being inside copying our "Fox" skeds I didn't know that Roper *had picked up a radar contact of some small vessel ahead of us and that we were investigating, nor did I know until after General Quarters sounded that our radar contact was a submarine which had launched at least one torpedo at us from its stern tubes. So after being relieved, I had just gotten below in the after living compartment when GQ sounded. Being just at the base*

Left to right: Rhodes Chamberlin, Jim Bunch and Roger Hunting talk about the *U-85*. Chamberlin was a member of the *Roper*'s crew and came back to scuba dive on the shipwreck. *Author's collection.*

of the after compartment ladder, I was the first man topside and out of the After Deck House on the starboard side just aft of the Number 5 gun. The 24-inch searchlight was illuminating a submarine about 300 yards off our starboard side. Number 5's 3inch gun was just starting to be manned as a half dozen or so men on the sub showed up on their deck heading for their guns, a 20mm on the conning tower and an 88mm forward. Almost immediately one of our 50 cal. machine guns on the Galley Deck House started firing, going back and forth as the sub sailors ran in and out from behind their conning tower as they tried to man their guns. Our Number 3 three inch on the Galley Deck House had misfired three times with a projectile jammed in the barrel on its last try. Meanwhile Chief Boatswains Mate Jack E. Wright who was manning the 50 cal. machine gun, which was right next to the No. 3 gun, continued firing back and forth on the sub deck with the sub sailors still trying to man their guns. By this time No. 5 was manned and Gun Captain Harry Heyman had his gun trained out and had started to fire. The third shell struck the sub at the base of the aft end of the conning tower. There was an explosion with a large spray of water, a sight I can still see plainly in my mind's eye. Moments later the sub started to sink, going down aft first. There were still only about 10 or 11 sailor's topside.

After watching a few more moments I went forward, arriving on the Well Deck, just as we approached, having continued our circling a group of survivors. I could see some of them just a few feet away. Someone called down from the bridge to release a large life raft, which was on a set of ways just overhead. I pulled the lanyard to release the raft when the small stuff which holds the center platform to the outer ring caught on the ways. I was in the process of cutting it loose when the bridge called down again to hold till next time around. Unfortunately a sound contact caused the decision to drop a pattern of depth charges which killed all of the survivors in the water. The next morning we picked up 29 bodies. Later that day they were transferred to the USS Scioto, which took them into NOB Norfolk.

I have often thought of the U-85 sinking and especially of the sight of our shell hitting the submarine. I have collected a number of accounts of it, all written by men who weren't there and all had some parts that were inaccurate. It took being contacted by Richard Reichenbacher who had dove on U-85 a number of times and was interested in my recollections of the sinking that really stirred my memories and gave me a very strong desire to revisit the scene.

So I got myself certified as an Open Water Diver and with Richard and Marty Bailey traveled to Nags Head. With the help of Jim and Beverly's Sea Scan Dive Center and Rich and Roger Hunting who gave us a boat ride, I was back where it all happened. Going down the line towards the U-85 and then having her come into view lying there on the bottom was a real thrill. Reaching the U-85's remains I was at last able to see and put my arm into the hole which 55 years before I had seen blown into U-85's hull that I still remember so vividly.

The Navy Visits the *U-85*

Within twenty-four hours after *U-85* went down, divers and equipment from the experimental diving unit in Washington, D.C., had been flown to the Naval Operations Base in Norfolk, Virginia, and were on board the British trawler HMS *Bedfordshire* steaming toward the spot where the U-boat was sunk. Since *U-85* was lying in about one hundred feet of water, the navy hoped that the sub could be refloated and salvaged.

HMS *BEDFORDSHIRE*

Arriving at position thirty-five degrees fifty-five minutes north, seventy-five degrees nineteen minutes west, and the orange marker buoy left by the *Roper*, the first diver was lowered from the *Bedfordshire* on April 16, 1942. The following day, diver number six found the *U-85*. Visibility was poor, and the diver could not identify what part of the boat he was on. Due to increasingly bad weather, no more attempts were made to reach the submarine during the next five days.

The *Bedfordshire*, on loan to the United States from Great Britain and soon to be sunk near Ocracoke, North Carolina, by the *U-558*, returned to convoy escort duty on April 20 and was replaced by the USS *Kewaydin*. Resuming diving operations from this ship on April 22, the second diver down found an unexploded American Mark VI depth charge lying next to the starboard side of the U-boat, again halting all diving until this charge was destroyed four days later by the navy's mine disposal unit.

HMS *Bedfordshire*. One of the ships sent to guard the salvage attempt on the *U-85*, the *Bedfordshire* was later sunk by *U-558* off Ocracoke Inlet with the loss of all hands. *Author's collection.*

USS *Falcon*

Seven more dives were made from the *Kewaydin*, and several buoyed lines were finally attached to the wreck before the diving and salvage vessel USS *Falcon* arrived at daybreak on Wednesday, April 29, 1942. With navy and coast guard escort vessels circling, World War I submarine veteran Bert Miller made the first dive to the *U-85* from the *Falcon* at noon on April 30. Miller, using a Mark V deep sea rig, dropped through the one hundred feet of water to the U-boat in about two minutes.

"When I reached the *85*, the sun was shining bright on it, and the first thing I saw was a wild boar's head with a rose in its mouth painted on the conning tower. The way the sun hit it, it was a beautiful sight underwater that I'll never forget. I wish I'd had a camera," Miller said. What Miller saw was the insignia painted on the U-boat by Lothar-Guenther Buchheim the previous summer.

Miller, whose dive lasted about one hour, made a visual inspection of the U-boat and found no major damage. He entered the conning tower and found the control room hatch closed but not dogged. Opening the hatch, he

USS *Falcon*, a diving and salvage vessel built in the early 1900s, arrived on the scene of *U-85*'s sinking on April 29, 1942. More than eighty dives were made from this ship to the *U-85* before leaving the site on May 4. *Bert Miller.*

Bert Miller, the first navy diver to reach the *U-85* from the USS *Falcon*, stands beside the graves of *U-85* crewmen at Hampton National Cemetery in Newport News, Virginia. *Author's collection.*

looked into the hatch and claimed that he was greeted by American money and Texaco oil cans floating in the flooded compartment.

During the next five days, seventy-eight dives were made to the *U-85* from the *Falcon*. Gauges, instruments, the 20mm antiaircraft gun from the bridge and the gun sight from the 88mm deck gun were removed. An attempt was also made to remove the aft torpedo storage container and torpedo, but this was unsuccessful. Several attempts to blow air into the diving and ballast tanks were also unsuccessful due to collapsed piping from depth charging.

On May 4, 1942, Lieutenant G.K. MacKenzie Jr., commanding officer aboard the *Falcon*, ended the diving operations after gathering the following information about the sunken U-boat: the *U-85* was listing about eighty degrees to starboard; all internal compartments were flooded with flood valves and vents open, except number two port and starboard, which was apparently secured as a reserve fuel tank; the forward torpedo tubes were loaded, with muzzle doors open; the hull and superstructure were undamaged except for holing by shell fire on the starboard side; the bow and stern planes were undamaged; the *U-85* was scuttled by its crew, and successful salvage could only be accomplished by extensive pontooning.

After recovering tools, mooring lines and anchors, the *Falcon* and its escort returned to the Naval Operations Base in Norfolk, Virginia, leaving only a large red buoy marked "A" attached to a quarter-inch line from *U-85*'s conning tower.

CHAPTER 10

MAY

The U-Boats Move South

The historian of the Eastern Sea Frontier wrote this about the month of May:

> *There was an extraordinary change this month in the fortunes of the war beneath the sea. April, when ships had gone down at the rate of almost one per day, was the worst month within the frontier since the submarine first invaded this coast. As it drew to a close there was no indication and no hope that these severe losses could be appreciably reduced in the foreseeable future. In fact when two vessels went down on the 30th of April it was possible to predict that sinking's might well increase. Then, in the first seventeen days of May not one ship was lost in the Eastern Sea Frontier.* [This excluded the escort vessels *Cythera* and *Bedfordshire*.] *In the fourteen days that remained of May only four vessels were sunk in our waters* [not off the North Carolina coast].

One VIIC, *U-352*, was also lost off Morehead City.

As the ASW forces slowly increased in number and ability north of Cape Lookout, Donitz continued to move more U-boats south to Florida where defenses were weaker.

U-459 at sea. Wolfgang Klue. *Author's collection.*

THE USS *CYTHERA* (PY 26)

The following history of the *Cythera* was compiled by Mike McCarthy:

The 600 ton Cythera was completed as the motor yacht Agawa. In October 1917 she was leased by the Navy and commissioned as patrol yacht USS Cythera. She was returned to her owner in March 1919. On 31 December 1941 she was bought by the US Navy for $1 from Edith H. Harkness, New York. She was converted to the patrol yacht USS Cythera (PY26) and commissioned on 3 March 1942.

USS Cythera, a small, wooden hull, converted yacht, was refitted in the Philadelphia Naval Ship Yard between December 1941 and March 1942. She was armed with two 3 inch deck guns, four .50 cal machine guns, and 50 depth charges and had a complement of five officers and 66 enlisted men. She was commanded by Cmdr. Charles Rudderow, a US Navy veteran of WW1. The boat was 212 feet long and had a 28 foot beam.

Around midnight on 1 May 1942, USS Cythera embarked from the US Navy Base in Norfolk, Virginia, enroute to Pearl Harbor, via Cristobal,

Panama Canal Zone. She was at sea only 24 hours, traveling south on a zigzag course, when she was attacked at 1 o'clock in the morning of May 2nd by U-402 *approximately 115 miles east of Cape Fear, North Carolina. The U-boat stalked the patrol vessel for at least two hours and finally submerged for an underwater attack. Von Forstner then fired three torpedoes in a fan shaped pattern. The first torpedo passed directly under the bow, the second passed under the stern, but the third struck the* Cythera *dead center. The ship immediately split in two and the forward half rose steeply out of the water. The ship sank very quickly and at least two of her depth charges that were preset exploded underwater. This information was told to me by one of the two survivors, Mr. James M. Brown, who I located in Maine in 1991. He was on forward lookout at the time of the attack. The other survivor was Charles H. Carter, but I was never able to locate him. He was standing on the bridge next to the commander when they were attacked. As a side note, Charles H. Carter was at Pearl Harbor aboard the battleship* USS Oklahoma *that was sunk during the Japanese attack. He survived two attacks within five months when the ships he was aboard were sunk.*

Shortly after the Cythera *went down,* U-402 *surfaced and turned on its search light looking at whatever debris was floating in the large oil slick that was all that remained from the ship. Brown and Carter were found clinging to a small raft and were taken aboard as prisoners. They asked to be left back in the water but Captain Von Forstner replied: No, boys, the war is over for you. Both survivors were covered in oil, and Von Forstner gave his sweater to Mr. Brown. Both were also given some brandy to drink. Brown also spoke fluent German, but I never thought to ask if he revealed that to Von Forstner. He did say, however, that the Chief Engineer on the U-boat spoke fluent English, so I suppose that's how they communicated. When Brown asked Von Forstner why they were not machine-gunned in the water, Von Forstner and the crew members present expressed shock that the Americans would even think such a thing.*

During the return trip to France the Americans were treated well. They were given cigarettes every day and allowed to go topside for fresh air every day. Brown said Von Forstner was a compassionate man who was not signed on to a Nazi ideology. He was a professional sailor who came from a family of military background. He was not enthusiastic about the war, but he did his job well as a German officer. When the Americans were turned over to the German Army in France there apparently was consternation between the U-boat crew and the German soldiers, who may have manhandled the POW's. In the almost three week trip to France, the crew and prisoners formed somewhat of a bond between them; in fact, the Americans even invited the crew to visit them in America after the war.

Brown, at least, wound up in a POW camp in Upper Silezia, Poland for the remainder of the war. The camp produced synthetic fuel and held mostly British POW's. Later in the war, the camp was abandoned because of advancing Soviet forces approaching from the east, and the POW's were force marched toward Moosburg, Germany to another camp. He was finally liberated in late April 1945 by forward units of Patton's 3rd Army and made his way back across Europe where he was put in a military hospital for several weeks.

U-352 AND HELLMUT RATHKE

Kapitanleutnant Hellmut Rathke would be one of the U-boat captains who brought his type VIIC boat, *U-352*, to the waters off the North Carolina coast in May 1942. Although he was a dedicated naval officer, he had to be one of the most inept U-boat commanders to visit the Americas. He and his crew would also have the distinction of being on board the second U-boat sunk off the Carolina coast. Not only would he be sunk by a boat that was much smaller and less well armed than he was, he would also demonstrate that all U-boat captains were not the cunning sea wolves they had been characterized to be.

Rathke's story begins when he left St. Nazaire on the morning of April 4 heading for American waters. He had been on one previous war cruise but sank no ships. It would be a relatively easy crossing, and he made it to American waters by May 4. Coming in off the New Jersey coast, he decided to head south and patrol the area where many of the boats had had good luck during the last several weeks. This spot, close to three hundred miles east of Cape Hatteras, would be far enough from the coast not to be patrolled by aircraft, and he could hunt on the surface during nighttime and daylight hours.

On the night of the fifth, Rathke began patrolling the new area for passing ships. He didn't have to wait long. Up from the southeast came a small freighter. What happened next is well told by writer Homer Hickham in his book *Torpedo Junction* and is summarized here. It is important in that it shows how the fortunes of war can change even when all seems lost.

Crew of the *U-352* soon after the commissioning ceremony on August 18, 1941. *Ed Caram.*

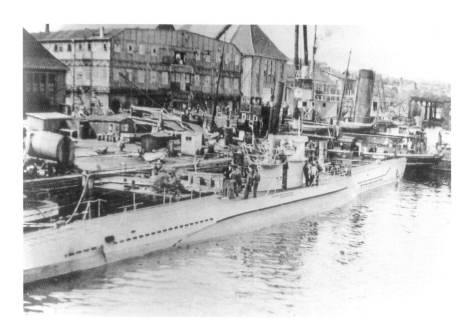

U-352 in Flensburg. *Ed Caram.*

About nine o'clock on May 5, under a bright moon, the small Swedish freighter *Freden* was proceeding along at about eight knots, heading right for the surfaced *U-352*. It would be an easy shot, and Rathke took it.

As the torpedo headed for the *Freden*, the lookout on the starboard side of the ship saw it coming and called out a warning. It was too late for the ship's helmsman to take action, but the torpedo missed and crossed the bow of the ship about one hundred feet ahead. Rathke saw the torpedo miss and ordered the *U-352* to motor ahead of the *Freden* for another try.

Within thirty minutes, Rathke was ready again. Still on the starboard side of the *Freden*, he fired the second torpedo. This one headed directly for the freighter as the starboard watch cried out again that another torpedo was on the way.

As the crewmen on board the ship prepared for the inevitable explosion, the watch on the port side cried out that the torpedo had exited his side of the ship. It had been set to run to deep and passed under the freighter.

The crewmen and the captain of the *Freden* had had enough. The ship was stopped, and everyone on board began to climb into the lifeboats and abandon ship. This went well, and soon they all were in the water.

For one reason or another, the captain now decided that maybe this wasn't such a good idea. They were three hundred miles out at sea and were leaving a perfectly good ship. He ordered all the crew to get back on board the *Freden*, started the engines and once again took off to the north at eight knots.

Rathke somehow didn't see the *Freden* stop and continued on north looking for it. He finally ordered the *U-352* to stop and thought he had lost it. After a while, one of the lookouts on the U-boat again spotted the *Freden* coming up from the south. He lined up for another shot, but this time he brought the U-boat in much closer. When the ship passed in front of him again, he fired torpedo number three at its starboard side.

Again the lookouts on the *Freden* saw it coming, and again it passed completely under the hull and came out the other side. The crew on the *Freden* were flabbergasted. How could a U-boat skipper be so stupid?

Rathke had not given up. He would try again. He moved ahead of the *Freden* and lined up, this time on the port side. He had the torpedo set for the shallowest draft on the scale. When the freighter moved directly in front of him, he fired the fourth bow torpedo at very close range.

The port side watch saw this one coming. Unlike the others, it was skipping across the water and passed in front of the bow. Rathke had wasted four torpedoes without a single hit.

The Swedish crew had definitely had enough this time. The freighter was again stopped and the ship abandoned. Rathke, who was now disgusted beyond belief, decided to let the freighter go, turned the *U-352* away and took off in the opposite direction.

The crew of the *Freden* saw the U-boat leave but decided to stay in their lifeboats. They drifted the rest of the night. When morning came, they were surprised to see the *Freden* drifting along beside them. They reboarded the ship and continued on to New York. Their adventures would be referred to as incredible by the navy intelligence officer who interviewed some of them.

SINKING OF THE *U-352*

Rathke brought the *U-352* close to the North Carolina coast on May 9 and settled on the bottom about twenty miles south of Cape Lookout to wait for nightfall. He had had no luck on his way in but knew that he was in a productive area based on what he had been told by other U-boat captains. Around four o'clock in the afternoon, he received his first alert from his chief radio man, Kurt Kruger. Kruger had heard the sound of an approaching ship that he estimated was only two thousand yards distant and making about ten miles an hour.

It was still daylight, and Rathke decided not to surface but to line up for a submerged attack. This was probably his first mistake.

As the unidentified ship came closer, Rathke, watching through his attack periscope in the conning tower, thought the steamer was a small merchant vessel. He realized the ship was smaller than the *U-352* but still decided to go ahead with a torpedo attack instead of surfacing and sinking the ship with his deck gun.

When the ship passed in front of Rathke, he fired one torpedo from his bow tube and waited. Within less than one minute, an explosion was heard by the sound operator on the U-boat, and Rathke ordered the sub back up to periscope depth. What he saw was not a burning freighter but the coast guard cutter *Icarus* bearing down on him. His torpedo had somehow malfunctioned and struck the sandy bottom over one hundred feet below the surface and exploded. The freighter was in fact the cutter *Icarus*. He had made his second mistake. This one would be fatal.

Rathke had to decide quickly what to do. He could surface and fight it out or stay down and hope for the best. He decided to stay down and move to the spot where his torpedo had exploded. He hoped the turbulence here would hide him from the *Icarus*.

This was another bad decision. The water depth here was only a little more than one hundred feet. The U-boat's conning tower would only be seventy feet below the surface, and if he had to run, the sub couldn't make enough headway to escape the *Icarus*. The U-boat was dead.

After hearing the torpedo explode, the sound man on the *Icarus* knew what to do. He could hear the propeller noise from *U-352* and knew where the boat was hiding. The commander of the *Icarus*, Lieutenant Commander Maurice D. Jester, quickly brought the cutter directly above the stationary U-boat and dropped his first pattern of depth charges.

The charges found their mark and all but destroyed the *U-352* with their devastating blasts. The first watch officer, Josef Ernst, who was in the conning tower, was killed immediately. The electric engines were wiped out, all power was lost and the 88mm deck gun was blown off the forward deck. Most of the instruments were put out of commission, and many of the crew were killed or critically injured.

The *Icarus* wasn't finished yet and continued to circle and drop more depth charges until the *U-352* finally blew all of its tanks and rose to the surface.

What happened next is well confirmed by both the German crewmen and the crewmen aboard the *Icarus*. The sub broke the surface, and the conning

Crew members of the sunken *U-352* on the docks in Charleston, South Carolina. *National Archives.*

Survivors of the German crew of the *U-352* are marched away from the dock in Charleston, South Carolina. *National Archives.*

tower hatch was opened. Rathke came out first, followed by an endless string of men. As they jumped into the water, the machine gun fire from the .50-caliber machine guns and the three-inch guns on the cutter cut many of them to pieces. Even after they were in the water and drifting away from the U-boat, the fire continued, killing them as they cried for mercy. Finally, the shooting stopped, and the cutter pulled away, leaving what was left of the U-boat crewmen drifting in the sea.

At first, it appeared that the crewmen would not be rescued at all but left to die in the ocean. Several messages were sent by the *Icarus* as to what should be done about the men in the water but were unanswered.

Finally, about thirty minutes after leaving the scene of the sinking, a message was received directing the *Icarus* to pick up the thirty-two survivors and bring them to Charleston, South Carolina, which Captain Jester did.

The thirty-two survivors, the first German U-boat men to be captured by Americans, were taken to an internment camp at Fort Bragg, North Carolina. With the sinking of the *U-352*, Rathke had lost a modern type VII U-boat, 220 feet long and capable of eighteen knots surfaced. The boat had fourteen torpedoes, a 20mm antiaircraft gun and an 88mm deck gun. He lost his boat to a 165-foot-long coast guard cutter with a three-inch gun, five .50-caliber machine guns and a few depth charges and only capable of a speed of sixteen knots.

The *Bedfordshire*

The HMS *Bedfordshire* was one of twenty-four armed trawlers sent to the United States to help fight the U-boats. It was a wooden vessel only 162 feet long and had previously been used for fishing. It was armed with one four-inch gun, a .303-caliber machine gun and seventy-five depth charges. Although British, it was under the control of the United States Navy and was no match for a German U-boat.

The boat had been one of the escorts that had guarded the spot where the *Roper* had sunk the *U-85* on April 14 and had since gone back to patrolling the coastline between Norfolk and Cape Lookout for U-boat activity. That's what it was doing on the night of May 12 when, just off Cape Lookout, a single torpedo fired by Gunther Krech from the *U-558* blew the wooden trawler to pieces. The blast was so sudden and devastating that no one on board had any chance of escape. All thirty-seven men on board were killed instantly.

The fate of the *Bedfordshire* was not discovered until May 14, when two bodies washed up on Ocracoke. They were soon identified by Dare County native Aycock Brown, who worked for the Office of Naval Intelligence. He knew one of the men personally and had had drinks with him not many days before. It was his friend Sub-lieutenant Thomas Cunningham. The two bodies were buried on Ocracoke Island on land donated by Mrs. Alice Williams near her family cemetery.

When May ended, the U-boat campaign along the American coast was failing. Something was needed to renew the victories that had been achieved over the past few months. Donitz had an idea, and he knew who could do it. It was Horst Degen, captain of the *U-701*. Degen had been the pupil of Captain Erich Topp and was one of the few commanders Donitz considered a favorite.

Degen met with Admiral Donitz in late May in his new office in Paris. Donitz wanted him to take six undercover saboteurs to America and then mine the harbor of Hampton Roads, Virginia. Degen let Donitz know that his boat would not be ready for several weeks but he would be honored to carry out this mission when the *701* was ready. Donitz replied that he would send the saboteurs on another boat but the mining operation could wait for him.

Degen left with his torpedo tubes loaded with fifteen mines on May 19 en route to America. His mission would go as planned except for one detail: he would lose his boat and most of his crew in early July.

CHAPTER 11

JUNE

An End in Sight

As June began, Karl Donitz realized that his investment of U-boats in American waters had been marginal in May but decided to continue his original plan for one more month. He had his hope that Captain Horst Degen and *U-701* could turn things around and his U-boats could still make a difference in the course of the war.

Although convoying, beginning with the Bucket Brigades and now evolving into full-scale ship escorting, had meant the end of the earlier successes, Donitz knew that large numbers of ships and men and unavoidable delays would result with the new system. He could still tie up large numbers of ASW forces with a small number of U-boats deployed along the East Coast.

Donitz would try it another month but began to send more boats south to the Caribbean Sea and the Gulf of Mexico, where defenses had not yet been established. He would also try new tactics, including Degen's mission of mining the Chesapeake Bay entrance and landing saboteurs along the East Coast of the United States. It would prove to be a futile effort.

JUNE RETURNS TO NEAR NORMAL
FOR MOST OUTER BANKERS

June began along the coast of North Carolina almost like it had the year before. The constant explosions of ships close to shore had ended, and the people along the coast felt a sense of relief that maybe it was all over. The

U-boats were staying well offshore and looking for targets several hundred miles at sea. Convoying of tankers and freighters was preventing the subs from finding lone targets and sinking them.

Jim Beasley, a resident of Kitty Hawk, remarked that it had been a nightmare but he thought it was over. He could get back to fishing and forget it all.

J.H. Wilkins, who owned several oceanfront cottages in Kitty Hawk, said he had never seen so many cans of drinking water wash up on the beach. They were gray in color and marked U.S. Navy.

Jim Scarborough, a native of Duck, said he was glad to get back to fishing and didn't mind the inconvenience, but he was glad it was over.

Jim Anderson, owner of Andersons Store in Kitty Hawk, said he was sorry for the losses folks had but he was ready to move on. His wife, Lula, said she hoped folks would come back to the beach and try to enjoy it.

The *West Notus*

June torpedo attacks opened more than three hundred miles off the coast of Cape Hatteras when Captain Otto von Bulow in the *U-404* attacked the freighter *West Notus*. He attacked the ship with his deck gun but was unable to sink it. After making sure all the crew were safely in lifeboats and away from the *Notus*, he finished the job with scuttling charges. He reportedly moved in close to the survivors and handed them a paper with directions and distance to Cape Hatteras written on it, wished them good luck and headed away on the surface.

Two days later, eighteen members of the crew were picked up by the freighter *Constantinos*. The following day, the rest were rescued by the *Saentis*.

The *Nordal*, the *Manuela* and the *Ljubica Matkovic*

Von Bulow traveled up and down the coast of North Carolina for twenty-three days and nights before he came across another ship to sink. Not only would he sink the *Nordal* with one torpedo at three o'clock in the morning of the twenty-fourth, but he would also sink two more ships, the *Manuela* and the *Ljubica Matkovic*, the following night near the same spot. Except for the two ships sunk by Horst Degen, no other vessels were sunk by U-boats off the coast of North Carolina in June.

With four victories to his credit in June, Otto von Bulow headed back to France that same night.

HORST DEGEN MINES THE CHESAPEAKE BAY ENTRANCE

After a difficult and stormy three-week crossing, Horst Degen and his *U-701* arrived at the mouth of the Chesapeake on the night of June 12. He had traveled mostly on the surface at five knots to conserve fuel and practiced crash diving the U-boat every day. Now he was here and ready to carry out his mission of placing fifteen mines on the sandy bottom of the channel between Cape Charles and Cape Henry. Here, in his own words, he tells about this historic event and his stay in American waters until he was sunk by a Lockheed Hudson on July 7:

> *Our task was to lay mines at the doorstep of Uncle Sam's own house. We had 15 magnetic ground mines, three in each tube. They were put into the tubes at Brest and were ready to be pushed out at Chesapeake Bay.*

U-701 in Kiel, Germany. Kapitanleutnant Horst Degan is second from right. *Ed Caram.*

As we approached the American coast, we were entertained by radio programs and the latest news from American radio stations. They did not know who they were entertaining. It was announced that it was June 12ᵗʰ, MacArthur's Day.

No airplanes or coast guard cutters greeted us as we neared the entrance to the bay. We could see the lights of Cape Henry and Cape Charles coming out from behind the skylight.

Our orders were to submerge near the channel in 36 feet of water and watch through our periscope during the day time the passage of ships in and out of the bay. We decided to do otherwise.

If the periscope were seen by an enemy ship while we were submerged in 36 feet of water, U-701 could be sunk or captured with all the secret material aboard.

We studied the chart we had and saw that there was only one way through the Bay to the City of Norfolk. A large sandbank extending from the Cape Charles side and required all ships entering to go to the south first and then around the tip and into the channel.

We would proceed at night into the channel and drop the fifteen mines in the 36 foot water one at a time. They would lay on the bottom for sixty hours before they became armed. Then when a ship passed over one of these mines it would explode and blow the bottom out of the ship.

So we started our journey into the channel. As we approached the Cape Henry side it was a breathtaking adventure to see cars and persons and lighted houses lining the beaches.

So now U-701 drew up into the channel where the eggs were to be laid. It was now one o'clock in the morning.

Now things began to happen. Through our night glasses we saw a trawler moving across the channel ahead of us from left to right. The trawler had no lights on because there was a war. The trawler gave way without knowing it and passed to the east of us.

Now we were at the place where our mine laying was to begin. The diesels were going slow ahead. Every minute the order was given to drop a mine.

We now switched to our electric motors because of the slight east wind and the trawler might hear the blup, blup, blup of our diesel motor.

About two A.M. our job was done. The second half of our mines had been laid and we headed out to the east. We had a feeling that the mines were laid in just the right position since we dropped them directly behind the trawler that was guarding the channel.

Nobody had been waiting for us half a mile outside the Naval Base in Norfolk Virginia. The new moon gave no light and a U-boat in the dark is very hard to see.

And so U-701 having done her job left the coast and took the deeper water. We submerged by early dawn so not to be discovered on our way out.

Now we reloaded our five torpedo tubes. This was done in about two hours after we submerged. Now that the four torpedoes up front had been pushed into their tubes, the sailors were able to rig a table and sit down for a meal.

That night we surfaced and ran at high speed for Cape Hatteras. We were now ready to hunt enemy ships with our torpedoes.

We still had to bring in the two torpedoes that were stored on the deck through the forward torpedo loading hatch. It took up about three hours to do this but we got through that job.

We reached Hatteras that first night of June 15th and looked around but didn't find much. That night we also received an order by wireless radio to stay submerged during the day because of the large number of American aircraft patrolling the coast there. So for the next few days we left the shallow water for the open ocean and about 300 feet of depth during the daytime. We stayed submerged during the day from about 6 am until 9 at night. It was summertime and a tremendous heat built up within the boat. The crew could hardly stand that. Nobody could know that this would bring the end to U-701 and most of her gallant crew in the near future.

It was the night of June 16th when we emerged and saw nothing thru the periscope. Three men and one watch officer took their places on the bridge. Nothing to see.

On the next nights we headed for Cape Lookout and Onslow Bay. All we saw were the remains of four large ships that had been sunk by our boats over the past four months. Their funnels and pilot houses stuck up above the water. No wonder there was no more traffic in the vicinity.

It became necessary now for us to emerge during the day around noon to clean the bad air out of the boat. We would emerge for about 15 minutes and let the running diesels clean the bad air out. This would be fatal for the U-701 later.

We decided to go out to a depth of close to 6000 feet and look for traffic. One morning we came up and observed a small vessel that looked like a trawler. She was a coast guard cutter painted blue with depth charges mounted on the stern. We did not want to waste our torpedoes on such a small ship.

The cutter went up and down and would not leave the area we were patrolling. The boat would march northward on a course of 40 degrees for about 10 miles and then turn around and head southward at 220 degrees. She was there to keep the shipping lanes open and scare U-boats away.

The next night we went out farther to try and get out of the path of this cutter. At 6 am we were again submerged and heading south away from the cutter.

About 10 am the radio operator heard propeller noises coming from the south. It was a tanker that was coming closer and would pass us at about 1000 meters.

The tanker coming up was one of the biggest tankers in the world. It was the William Rockefeller *loaded with 140,000 barrels of fuel oil from Aruba and heading for New York. After being torpedoed, the entire 44 man crew escaped the burning ship and were quickly picked up by the escorts.*

U-701 had the perfect position. Two torpedoes were fired and a big explosion occurred amid ship. The tanker was burning all over. Suddenly three heavy explosions of depth charges let us know that somebody was there to take care of us.

William Rockefeller in flames. *Ed Caram.*

We ran away and came up to periscope depth to see two destroyers guarding the burning tanker. By nightfall they left and disappeared into the dusk. We moved close to the tanker and realized it was the 14,500 ton ship William Rockefeller. *We had to give her one more torpedo for the kill.*

One torpedo was fired at 1 am and hit the engine room. The ship stood up on its stern with a tremendous fireball shooting skyward like a terrible nightmare. She then went down by the stern in a giant slide hissing all over instantly and then all was dark. U-701 *found herself alone in the sea. It was as somebody had switched off the lights.*

The next day there was the cutter again. Again we could not emerge. We waited at her southern point of turning around and heading north again. We had decided to come up behind her and get her with our artillery.

It was about midnight when the cutter emerged heading on 240 degrees again and then turned and started back on 40 degrees northward.

Those brave men on that ship could not have known that they were doomed the next hour.

U-701 *slowly pulled up behind. Like a shadow coming up in the darkness we changed our course to 60 degrees to clear the path of our guns and then opened up with 88mm cannon fire and 20mm flak fire on the poor vessel.*

The cutter tried to answer our attack but was unable to do it. First she turned to starboard in an attempt to ram us and then to port in a large circle. In the blazing flames we could not recognize any one alive on the ship. A brave crew and a brave ship had ceased to exist.

About 40 years later I got notice that the name of the ship was YP-389. *Almost the whole crew was saved because they hid on the other side of the bridge so it was not so dramatic for them. The Captain of the ship was however accused of not attacking us properly and I think was Court-Martialed. He could not see us coming and it was not his fault.*

Later that night we received a radio message from Admiral Donitz telling us that according to an intercepted enemy wireless, 4 ships and 1 destroyer had gone down as a result of our mines in Chesapeake Bay. Well done says Donitz.

What the mines had done is described by Clair Blair in his book *Hitler's U-Boat War: The Hunters, 1939–1942*. In the late afternoon of June 15, a coastal convoy from Key West, KN 109, composed of twelve ships and six escorts, arrived off the entrance to Chesapeake Bay. At about that same time, Degen's mines, delayed for sixty hours, activated. As the convoy

YP-389, February 14, 1942, at the Navy Yard in Brooklyn, New York, undergoing conversion from the *Cohasset*. *National Archives.*

moved into Norfolk, it passed directly over Degen's field. The mines severely damaged two big, loaded American tankers, *R.C. Tuttle* and *Esso Augusta*, and destroyed the five-hundred-ton British ASW trawler *Kingston Celoynite*, which was escorting the freighter *Delisle*, damaged earlier in Florida waters by Scotty Suhren in *U-564*. Seventeen of the thirty-two-man British crew on the trawler perished.

Believing at first that these ships had been torpedoed, the convoy escort, including the four-stack destroyer *Bainbridge* and the 165-foot coast guard cutters *Dione* and *Calypso*, ran about madly throwing off depth charges. One of Bainbridge's missiles detonated another German mine, which damaged it, but only slightly. Two days later, on June 17, another of the mines blew up the outbound 7,100-ton American freighter *Santore*, which could not be salvaged. Upon hearing incorrectly from B-dienst that these mines had sunk four merchant ships and a destroyer, Donitz radioed Degen a "well done" and ordered him to patrol the dangerous waters off Cape Hatteras.

YP-389. National Archives.

Robert C. Tuttle on fire after being damaged by one of *U-701*'s mines inside Chesapeake Bay. *National Archives.*

The next days and nights we hung around Hatteras but were not able to emerge at noon for fresh air. It was the time of the full moon and we merrily rode around at night looking for enemy shipping. In the moonlight a submarine can be easily seen on the glistening surface of the sea because he is creating a black streak.

So one night an airplane spotted us on the surface and came over us at fifty feet. We never saw the airplane because he came from the dark side. We only heard it. The bombs were five depth charges but they failed to hit us. We knew now that we had to be careful in the moonlight and had to take good care.

CHAPTER 12

JULY

The U-Boats Are Recalled
from the Coast of North Carolina

When July began, Admiral Karl Donitz and his staff officer of U-boat operations, Fregattenkapitan Gunther Hessler, came to some conclusions about continuing the offensive along the U.S. coast. The following summary of why Donitz took the action he did was written after the war at the British Admiralty's request by Gunther Hessler:

> *In early July, very few U-boats were still operating off the North Carolina Coast. Those that were still here were assigned to patrol areas close to shore. An attempt was made to control operations from U-boat headquarters which had proved to be very successful in the past. This would no longer be the case now.*
>
> *It was thought possible that coastal traffic would increase during the full-moon period during early July, when the U-boats would be unable to operate near the coast because of the bright moonlight. If this proved to be correct it would be uneconomical to continue operations near the U.S. coast.*
>
> *The situation appeared to change when in early July, a number of small convoys and escorted single vessels were sighted near Cape Hatteras. U-701 and U-404 commanded by experienced officers Degen and Bulow managed to sink a few ships near Cape Hatteras while at the same time two fast vessels were sunk 200 miles at sea. It was evident that the fewer sightings were attributable not to the suspension or diversion of traffic, but to the introduction of the convoy system. Because of these successful convoy attacks the boats were kept in the Hatteras area.*

It was hoped that the sighting boat would be able to direct several other boats to the attack. Three more convoys were sighted but the plan failed on each occasion. The problem was that the sighting boat could not reach the attacking position because of strong enemy air cover.

U-701 and U-404 had owed their success in the past to their favorable position ahead of the convoys. Such chances would probably recur when the volume of traffic increased and it seemed worth trying this for a while longer.

It didn't work out this way. From mid-July nearly all our boats were being attacked from the air, and the damage caused to both U-87 and U-404 by constant bombing forced them to leave the area.

By mid-July, U-701 and U-576 had been sunk. These losses, representing one third of the forces engaged here were not commensurate the results we needed to stay. On July 19th the two boats still operating near Cape Hatteras were ordered to evacuate the coastal areas. Thus the increasing ascendancy of the American A/S forces drove us from the United States Coast. In the future we would send only single boats there occasionally, and perhaps to lay mines off some of the major ports.

The Sinking of *U-701*

Degen's testimonial continues:

At dawn on July 7th U-701 submerged again along the 300 meter line. This day was not to bring a victorious sinking of enemy ships but doom for U-701 and her crew.

At one o'clock pm we went up, looked through the periscope and no enemy ships were about. The sky was clear of airplanes. It was sunny day with a few clouds up high. Water depth under the boat was about 270 feet. A little east of our position the bottom would go down to three thousand feet, it was only a few miles. By sheer luck we went west instead of east. If we had gone east all of us would have died with the plunge to the bottom. When we emerged for air renewal we blew all tanks, and ran the diesels full speed ahead. Three good lookouts and the skipper dashed up to the bridge in case some enemy would show up. The ship rushed forward in the fresh breeze and filled the rooms with cool air. No ships or airplanes were around. After about 5 minutes on the surface the engineering officer gave the signal that the sub was alright with fresh air. Let's take her down again. Take her down, the hissing noise of the air leaving the tanks and the diesel engines stopped and U-701 began to settle below the surface. Two of the watch had already jumped down the hatch. Now the third man jumped down and cried airplane coming in from 200 degrees port aft. As he fell down the hatch the skipper had already taken a terrified look in that direction. And before he could close the conning tower hatch with water flowing over it he saw a four motor liberator. But it was not a liberator but a Lockheed Hudson Bomber that had dashed down from under a cloud. U-701 managed her best diving and in no time she was at 90 feet. The crew was given a short word as what was about to happen. It was silent in the sub. Only the electric motors that were running at full speed gave their singing melody. The watch officer received a scolding for not seeing the plane in time. We reached 105 feet depth and then it happened. We hear two roaring explosions at the stern. Two depth charges had hit us and must have ripped the aft hull to pieces. An overwhelming water flood came thru the door from the aft. Blow all tanks but that could not work anymore. The tanks were blown but the sub went down due to the heavy water tumbling in from the engine room. The instruments showed 120 feet when our deadly wounded submarine was thrown to the bottom of the ocean. The water rose and within a few minutes water was all the way up to the top of the conning tower. There was no connection with the other rooms and only 30 cm. of air below the ceiling. I said everyone get out of here abandon ship. The heat grew worse. It was total catastrophe. The main conning tower hatch was opened by the skipper and he was thrown toward the surface as the compressed air took him up. Then the way out was free for all. Soon there were about sixteen men on the surface. Above our heads there was still the Lockheed Hudson. They threw us two life rafts but they drifted away. We thought we would be rescued soon. We kept on swimming thru the afternoon and waited for rescue. As the afternoon went on some of the men went down due for exhaustion. Two other men took off in a west direction. We never saw them again. Just before sunset we could see a large convoy of ships passing by. We were 12 men left hanging on to six lifebelts. The night went pretty fast and the next morning a coast guard speed boat came toward us. We waved our arms but it was all in vein [sic]. They passed us by at about 1000 yards. Later we found out that they were looking for us. As the day went by more men gave up. During the day there were only seven men left in our group. The murderous thirst gave us hallucinations. We did find a lemon and a coconut. Each of us had a taste of the milk and a piece of

U-701 survivors are carried from the coast guard rescue plane at Norfolk Naval Air Station. *National Archives.*

Horst Degen (*fourth from left*) and the other survivors of the *U-701* pose with the coast guard pilot who saved them. *National Archives.*

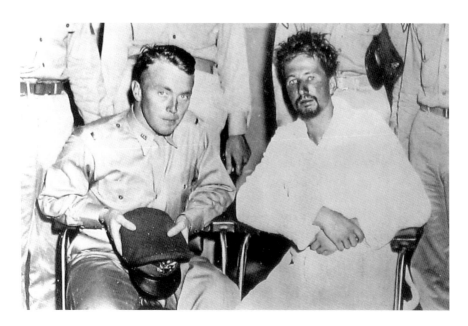

Harry Kane visits with Horst Degen at the Naval Hospital in Norfolk, Virginia. *National Archives.*

the lemon. July 8th ended with only a few of us alive. Now it became very cold in the water. We lost one man that night. On the morning of July 9th there were only four of us left. We were all almost gone. At noon a blimp of the U.S. Navy sighted us and came over at 90 feet. They dropped us a raft and three men climbed in. The men in the blimp pointed to one more man in the water close by. They got him in the boat too. It was Capt. Horst Degen. The blimp threw us water and blankets and left. About an hour later a sea plane came down and came close to us. They shouted come over here. Well we paddled over and we were taken into the plane. Now came the big surprise. They had also picked up three men from our forward torpedo room. Only three of about 20 men who got out swam for about 50 hours and survived. The sea plane took off for Norfolk Va. We had swam about 90 sea miles. The bomber crew visited us the next day. The pilot Harry Kane came from the 396 at Cherry Point airport. We never saw freedom again until June 6, 1946.

Convoy KS-520 and the *U-576*

The only true convoy battle that took place off the North Carolina coast was that between *U-576*, captained by Hans-Dieter Heinicke, and the ships of KS-520.

Heinicke was already patrolling the area around Cape Lookout and wasn't aware of KS-520's sailing date. On July 12, he had spotted a smaller convoy near Cape Lookout heading north. He trailed the convoy for some distance but could not get close enough to attack. He also tried to vector in the other boat in the area, Siegfried Von Forstner in *U-402*, but was unsuccessful. After reporting his dilemma to Kerneval, he and Von Forstner were both ordered to take up positions near Cape Hatteras.

During the next two days, both U-boats were attacked from the air by aircraft, and on July 13, Heinicke reported to Kerneval that he had sustained damage from aircraft and was attempting repairs. Von Forstner reported the same situation. Heinicke indicated that he could not fix his problems and was heading home. Von Foster was told to move east four hundred miles out of the range of ASW aircraft and attempt to repair his boat.

The nineteen-ship convoy gathered in Chesapeake Bay on July 12 and 13, 1942. Tankers, freighters and ore carriers were included in the large assortment of ships preparing to sail together. A full escort of two destroyers, two patrol boats, two coast guard cutters and one corvette would guard the group the whole way to Key West, Florida. One navy blimp and two planes from the Norfolk Naval Air Station would provide air cover. The nineteen ships in the convoy were *Mount Pera*, *Bluefields*, *Zouave*, *Tustem*, *Gulf Prince*, *Robert H. Colley*, *American Fisher*, *Para*, *Mount Helmos*, *Jupiter*, *Hardanger*, *Nicania*, *Toteco*, *Clam*, *Egton*, *J.A. Mowinckel*, *Unicoi*, *Rhode Island* and *Chilore*. The five support vessels that made up the escort were USS *Ellis*, USS *McCormick*, USS *Spry*, USCG *Triton* and USCG *Icarus*. Several of the merchant vessels in the convoy also had armed guard crews aboard manning deck guns. Captain Newton Nichols, USN, was the convoy commander and took his place aboard the tanker *Mowinckel*.

The convoy departed the bay early on July 14 and formed into seven columns once in the ocean. The escorts fanned out around the ships, with the destroyers taking a lead and trailing position. The sea was calm, and the group of twenty-six ships moved along toward the south at about eight knots.

By the afternoon of the fifteenth, the group had made it past Cape Hatteras and had turned southwestward toward Ocracoke. Two pilots from

U-576 at sea. *Author's collection.*

Cherry Point Marine Corps Air Station showed up to relieve the planes from Norfolk that had been providing air cover up until now.

Heinicke and *U-576* were still in the area and apparently spotted the approaching convoy. Unable to resist attacking even in his damaged condition, he took up a firing position ahead of the large group of ships.

The coast guard cutter *Triton* had just chased down a contact, probably *U-576*, and was in the process of dropping depth charges when the planes arrived. Not long after the charges exploded, the pilots saw a torpedo heading for the leading tanker in the second column. The tanker, *Chilore*, was struck on its port bow and stopped dead in the water.

In less than a minute, the lead ship in the fourth column, *Mowinckel*, was also hit on the port side. Seconds later, the freighter *Bluefields* was hit. A fourth torpedo barely missed the *Unicoi* by several hundred feet. The *U-576* had fired all four of its bow torpedoes in rapid succession and scored three hits.

The aircraft pilots were amazed to now see the U-boat very near the burning ships, still submerged but very close to the surface. Apparently, the

U-576 was the last U-boat to go down off the North Carolina coast. *Ed Caram.*

Bluefields, sunk near Cape Hatteras by *U-576*. *National Archives.*

release of all four three-thousand-pound torpedoes had made the sub too light, and it had floated almost to the surface.

One of the pilots, Ensign Frank Lewis, immediately lined the *U-576* up and began his attack. He came in at less than one hundred feet and 130 miles per hour, dropping two depth charges that both went off on either side of the sub. Ensign Charles Webb followed behind Lewis and dropped his charges, which hit the submarine near the conning tower.

U-576 was probably fatally damaged at this point but managed to stay afloat with its bow rising out of the water. Its conning tower, which had been submerged, was also now exposed.

The armed guard on the *Unicoi* had been watching all of this, and when the sub came up only three hundred yards from them, they opened up, with their four-inch gun hitting *U-576* in the conning tower. They kept firing and continued firing until the sub's stern rose almost vertically from the water and *U-576* and its crew went down for the last time. The destroyer *Ellis* steamed toward the spot where the sub went down and dropped depth charges in the more than six hundred feet of water. An oil slick soon appeared on the surface.

The U-boat war off the coast of North Carolina was, for all practical purposes, over.

CHAPTER 13

THE COST WAS HIGH

During the months of January through July 1942, more than seventy ships were sunk by German U-boats off the coast of North Carolina. With them, over 1,700 merchant seamen and civilian passengers lost their lives. The Germans paid a price also, but it was small in comparison to the havoc they created. Four U-boats were destroyed with the loss of 165 crewmen.

Looking at the part U-boats played during the entirety of World War II, the following facts show just how large it was.

Germany started the war in September 1939 with 57 U-boats. During the course of the war, 1,153 boats were built and commissioned. Contracts were placed for another 1,153, but they were never finished.

Of the boats that were commissioned, 830 took part in just over three thousand operations, sinking more than 3,500 ships worldwide totaling more than eighteen million tons. Over 500 of the boats commissioned sank nothing; 290 of these were sunk without firing a torpedo.

The greatest number of U-boats that were in operation at one time during the war occurred in January 1944, when 456 were available. More boats were actually at sea in May 1943, when 120 were engaged in combat. The most sinkings in a single month occurred in March 1942 and amounted to around 830,000 tons. The greatest number of U-boats sunk in one month occurred in April 1945 with 64 destroyed.

To summarize, of the 1,153 boats commissioned, 636 were destroyed by enemy depth charges, bombs, mines, torpedoes, guns and bombs; 63 by air

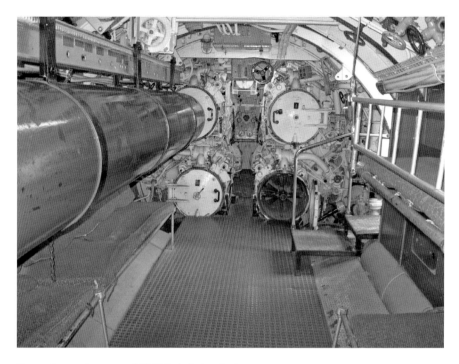

Forward torpedo room of *U-995. Author's collection.*

attack on U-boat bases and shipyards; and 85 through accidents, internal explosions, collision and other causes, for a total loss of 784.

On May 4, 1945, all U-boats at sea were ordered to cease hostilities and return to base. Many of the captains, contrary to the order, scuttled their boats where they were. A total of 218 went down in this way. This left only 154 U-boats in various places that were surrendered to the Allies on May 9 when Germany's surrender came into force, and only 43 of these boats were at sea. Of the few that remained, 110 were towed into the deep waters northwest of Ireland and sunk by the British between November and February 1946. The few retained by the United States and other Allies soon met a similar fate. The two exceptions are the *U-995*, which was eventually returned to Germany and remains on display across from the German Naval Memorial at Laboe, and the *U-505*, on display at the Chicago Museum of Science and Industry.

BIBLIOGRAPHY

Books

Bagnasco, Erminio. *Submarines of World War Two*. Annapolis, MD: Naval Institute Press, 1977.

Beaver, Paul. *U-boats in the Atlantic*. Cambridge, UK: Patrick Stephens Limited, 1979.

Blair, Clay, Jr. *Hitler's U-boat War*. Vols. 1 and 2. New York: Random House, 1997.

Bottling, Douglas. *The U-boats*. Fairfax, VA: Time Life Books, 1979.

Breyer, Siegfried, and Gerhard Koop. *The U-boat*. Atglen, PA: Schiffer Publishing, 1987.

Bucheim, Gunther. *U-boat War*. N.p.: Bonanza Books, 1986.

Bunch, Jim. *Diving the U-85*. N.p.: Deep Sea Press, 1986.

———. *U-85: A Shadow in the Sea*. N.p.: Deep Sea Press, 2003.

Bush, Rainer, and Hans-Joachim Roll. *German U-boat Commanders of World War II*. Barnsley, UK: Greenhill Books, 1999.

Caram, Ed. *Fires Along the Coast*. N.p., n.d.

———. *U-352: The Sunken German U-boat in the Graveyard of the Atlantic*. N.p., 1987.

Cheatham, James T. *The Atlantic Turkey Shoot: U-boats Off the Outer Banks in World War Two*. Barnsley, UK: Greenhill Books, 1999.

Chewning, Alpheus J. *The Approaching Storm: U-boats off the Virginia Coast During World War Two*. Richmond, VA: Brandylane Publishers, 1994.

Cremer, Peter. *U-boat Commander*. Annapolis, MD: Naval Institute Press, 1984.

Duffus, Kevin. *War Zone*. Milwaukee, WI: Looking Glass Productions, 2012.

Edwards, Bernard. *Donitz and the Wolf Pacts*. Leicester, UK: Brockhampton Press, 1999.

Farb, Roderick. *Shipwrecks: Diving the Graveyard of the Atlantic.* Birmingham, AL: Menasha Ridge Press, 1985.

Gannon, Michael. *Black May.* New York: Dell Publishing, 1998.

———. *Operation Drumbeat.* New York: Harper and Row, 1990.

Gasaway, E.B. *Grey Wolf Grey Sea.* New York: Ballantine Books, 1970.

Gentile, Gary. *Shipwrecks of North Carolina (North).* N.p.: Gary Gentile Publications, 1993.

———. *Shipwrecks of North Carolina (South).* N.p.: Gary Gentile Publications, 1992.

———. *Track of the Grey Wolf.* New York: Avon Books, 1989.

Geroux, William. *The Mathews Men.* New York: Viking, 2016.

Heinz, Karl, and Michael Schmeelke. *German U-boat Bunkers.* Atglen, PA: Schiffer Publishing, 1999.

Hickam, Homer H. *Torpedo Junction.* Annapolis, MD: Naval Institute Press, 1989.

Hogel, Georg. *U-boat Emblems of World War Two 1939–1945.* Atglen, PA: Schiffer Publishing, 1999.

Hoyt, Edwin P. *U-boats: A Pictorial History.* New York: McGraw-Hill, 1987.

Hughes, Terry, and John Costello. *The Battle of the Atlantic.* New York: Dial Press, 1977.

Irving, David. *The Destruction of Convoy PQ17.* New York: Simon and Schuster, 1968.

Jones, Geoffrey. *Defeat of the Wolfpacks.* N.p.: William Kimber and Co., 1991.

Kahn, David. *Seizing the Enigma.* Boston: Houghton Mifflin Company, 1991.

Kaplan, Philip, and Jack Currie. *Wolfpack U-boats at War 1939–1945.* Annapolis, MD: Naval Institute Press, 1997.

Keatts, Henry, and George Farr. *Dive into History: U-boats.* N.p.: Pices Books, 1994.

Kutta, Timothy. *U-boat War.* N.p.: Squadron Signal Publications, 1998.

Macintyre, Donald. *The Naval War Against Hitler.* New York: Scribner's Sons, 1971.

Mason, David. *U-boat: The Secret Menace.* New York: Ballantine Books, 1969.

Miller, David. *U-boats: The Illustrated History of the Raiders of the Deep.* N.p.: Pegasus Publishing Ltd., 2000.

Mulligan, Timothy P. *Lone Wolf: The Life and Death of U-boat Ace Werner Henke.* N.p.: Prager, 1993.

———. *Neither Sharks nor Wolves.* Annapolis, MD: Naval Institute Press, 1999.

Naiswald, L. VanLoan. *In Some Foreign Field.* Winston-Salem, NC: John F. Blair, 1972.

Niestle, Axel. *German U-boat Losses During World War Two.* Annapolis, MD: Naval Institute Press, 1992.

Nowarra, Heinz. *The German U-boat Type VII.* Atglen, PA: Schiffer Publishing, 1992.

Ott, Wolfgang. *Sharks and Little Fishes*. New York: Ballantine Books, 1970.

Pitt, Barrie. *The Battle of the Atlantic: World War II*. Fairfax, VA: Time Life, 1977.

Porten, Edward. *The German Navy in World War II*. N.p.: Thomas Crowell, 1969.

Preston, Anthony. *U-boats*. Lincoln, NE: Bison Books, 1978.

Robertson, Terrance. *The Golden Horseshoe*. N.p.: Evans Brothers Ltd., 1955.

Roessler, Eberhard. *The U-boat*. Annapolis, MD: Naval Institute Press, 1984.

Rohwar, Jurgen. *Axis Submarine Successes, 1939–1945*. Annapolis, MD: Naval Institute Press, 1984.

Roscoe, Theodore. *United States Destroyer Operations in World War II*. Annapolis, MD: Naval Institute Press, 1953.

Savas, Theodore P. *Silent Hunters: German U-boat Commanders of War II*. N.p.: Savas Publishing Company, 1977.

Showell, J.P. Mallmann. *The German Navy in World War Two*. Annapolis, MD: Naval Institute Press, 1979.

———. *U-boat in Camera*. Stroud, UK: Sutton Publishing, 1999.

———. *U-boats Under the Swastika*. N.p.: Arko, 1974.

Stern, Robert C. *Type VII U-boats*. Leicester, UK: Brockhampton Press, 1991.

———. *U-boats in Action*. N.p.: Squadron/Signal Publications, 1977.

Stick, David. *Graveyard of the Atlantic*. Chapel Hill: University of North Carolina Press, 1952.

———. *The Outer Banks of North Carolina*. Chapel Hill: University of North Carolina Press, 1958.

Suhren, Teddy. *Teddy Suhren, Ace of Aces*. Annapolis, MD: Naval Institute Press, 2006.

Tarrant, V.E. *The U-boat Offensive 1914–1945*. Annapolis, MD: Naval Institute Press, 1989.

Terraine, John. *The U-boat War, 1916–1945*. N.p.: Henry Holland Company, 1989.

Topp, Erich. *The Odyssey of a U-boat Commander*. N.p.: Prager, 1992.

U-boat Commanders Handbook. Gettysburg, PA: Thomas Publications, 1989.

Vause, Jordan. *U-boat Ace: The Story of Wolfgang Luth*. Annapolis, MD: Naval Institute Press, 1990.

———. *Wolf: U-boat Commanders in World War II*. Annapolis, MD: Naval Institute Press, 1997.

Waters, Captain John M., USCG, retired. *Bloody Winter*. Annapolis, MD: Naval Institute Press, 1984.

Werner, Herbert A. *Iron Coffins*. New York: Holt, Rinehart & Winston, 1969.

Westwood, David. *The Type VII U-boat*. Annapolis, MD: Naval Institute Press, 1984.

Wiggins, Melanie. *U-boat Adventures*. Annapolis, MD: Naval Institute Press, 1999.

Wynn, Kenneth. *U-boat Operations of the Second World War*. Vol. 1. Annapolis, MD: Naval Institute Press, 1997.

Unpublished Material

National Archives II. Adelphi, Maryland

Record Group 38
The records of the Office of Naval Intelligence, located among the Records of the Chief of Naval Operations, Record Group 18, include several sources of information. The records of the Office Op., responsible during World War II for intelligence about German U-boat activities, includes copies of paper records and personal effects recovered from the bodies of *U-85* crewmen, as well as detailed data on the identification and internment of the remains of the *U-85* crew.

Record Group 80-G
Photos of the bodies recovered from the *U-85* can be found in Box 64. There are about fifty different shots, both on the *Roper* and in the cemetery.

Record Group 242
Microfilm Publication T1022. Records of the German navy, 1850–1945. *U-85*'s Kriegstabrbuch (KTB), June 7, 1941–April 8, 1942, is reproduced on microfilm publication T1002, rolls 2931-32, as record item PG30079/1-5. The microfilm is available in the microfilm research room on the fourth floor.

Records of the Tenth Fleet
Among the records of the U.S. Tenth Fleet, which coordinated anti-submarine operations during the war, there is a detailed account of *U-85*'s sinking by the USS *Roper* among the ASW assessment files (Incident No. 400), including the *Roper*'s own after-action report of the sinking. Finally, a collection of intercepts of decrypted and translated German navy messages includes a number of messages sent or received by the *U-85* in late 1941 and early 1942.

INDEX

About the Author

J im Bunch is the leading authority on the *U-85*, the first German U-boat sunk by a United States warship after America's entry into World War II. He's done more than one thousand dives to the *U-85* and is the author of *Diving the U-85* and *U-85: A Shadow in the Sea, a Diver's Reflections*. An accomplished teacher, speaker, writer and underwater photographer, Bunch started diving the shipwrecks of North Carolina's Outer Banks in the mid-1950s. Specializing in oceanography, he earned degrees in marine biology (BS) and oceanography (MS) and worked as an oceanographer for the federal government for many

years while pursuing his diving interests. As a former dive business owner and an NAUI scuba instructor for eighteen years, he equipped and certified hundreds of divers interested in visiting North Carolina's shipwrecks. In 1994, he received the Scuba Schools International Pro 5000 award for making five thousand or more logged open-water dives. Bunch is a Road Scholar speaker with the North Carolina Humanities Council, a past chairman of NOAA's Monitor Marine Sanctuary Advisory Council and serves on the board of Friends of the Graveyard of the Atlantic Museum.